SPECTRUM
Sight Words

Grade K

Spectrum
An imprint of Carson-Dellosa Publishing LLC
P.O. Box 35665
Greensboro, NC 27425 USA

Printed in the USA • All rights reserved.   ISBN 0-7696-6680-9

2 3 4 5 6 7 8 PAH 13 12 11 10   12010016335

Table of Contents

Notes to Parents and Teachers

Whenever a young child reads, 50 to 75% of the words he or she comes across are from the Fry Instant Sight Word List. This is a highly respected, research-based list of the 300 most frequently used words in the English language. Typically, these high-frequency words do not follow regular phonics patterns or spelling rules, making them very difficult for young children to sound out or decode. Consequently, learning to recognize these words immediately "by sight" is a critical first step to successful, confident, fluent reading.

Spectrum Sight Words for Kindergarten, and its companion, *Spectrum Sight Words for Grade 1*, introduce, practice, and review all of the words on this list to help children develop sight word mastery, confidence, and fluency as they encounter these words in both reading and writing. *Spectrum Sight Words* are intended for use in school programs or at home with 5-, 6-, and 7-year-olds. The contents are also suitable for older children needing more practice, or for younger children developing early reading skills.

Follow these helpful steps when using this book:
- Follow the exact sequence of the book's exercises, as each sight word is introduced—and then reviewed—in its specific order on the Fry Instant Sight Word List, beginning with the most frequently appearing words.
- Encourage your child to work at his or her own pace, and offer support and praise as he or she completes the exercises.
- Take advantage of the blank flash cards to personalize your child's flash card set.
- Review and evaluate sight word memory by using the sight word flash cards at the back of the book.
- Use the tracing flash cards for added assistance in discriminating, reading, and writing the sight words.
- Help your child develop and demonstrate sentence sense by using the sentence strip activities to recognize sight words in correct sentence order.

As teachers and parents, it is our goal to support and foster the learning of all of our children. Activities and materials in *Spectrum Sight Words for Kindergarten* help meet those needs by promoting the appropriate pacing and challenge that allows each child to master reading success.

Target words: the, I, like

Directions: Say each word as you trace it. Then, write each word on the line.

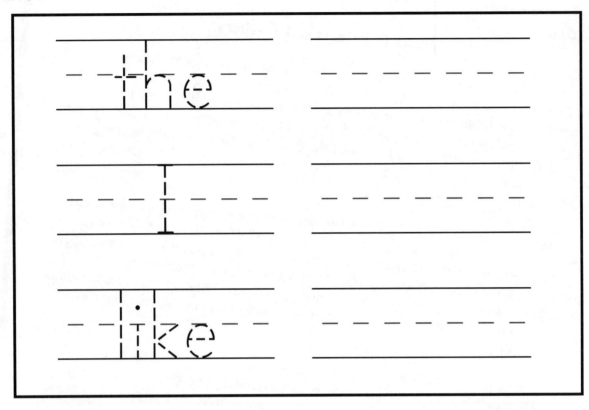

Directions: Color the boxes that have these words in them:

I   the   like

the	like	long	I
in	it	the	like
like	I	in	that
then	look	I	the

Target words: the, I, like

Directions: Write the missing word in each sentence.

| I | the | like |

1. _____ want to play.

2. Do you _____ dogs?

3. Where is _____ cat?

Directions: Find and circle the word **like**. It can go → or ↓.

l	i	k	e	b	r
i	t	l	i	k	e
k	l	i	k	e	x
e	z	k	w	p	v
m	o	e	a	d	c

How many did you circle? _____

Target words: **to, here**

Directions: Say each word as you trace it. Then, write each word on the line.

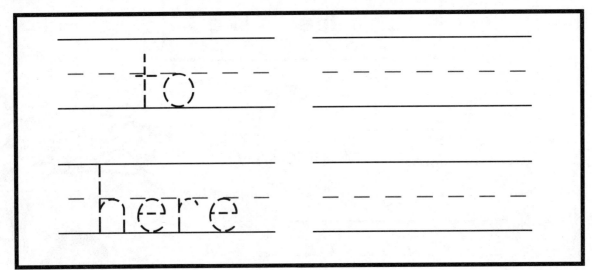

Directions: Say each word as you write each sentence.

I like to play ball.

_____

— — — — — — — — — — — — — — —

_____

Throw the ball here.

_____

— — — — — — — — — — — — — — —

_____

Target words: **to, here**

Directions: Draw a railroad track to connect the words that rhyme.

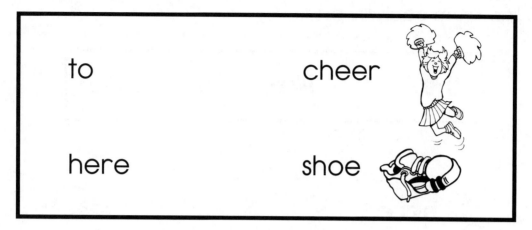

to   cheer

here   shoe

Directions: Look for the words **to** and **here** in each track. Circle them each time you see them.

Target words: the, I, like, to, here

Directions: Help the frog cross the pond. Find these words and draw a line from each lily pad.

| the | I | like | to | here |

here

is

to

look

like

then

my

on

I

the

it

Target words: **is, a, and**

Directions: Write the missing word in each sentence.

is	a	and

_____

1. This _____ a monkey.

_____

2. This is _____ cat.

_____

3. Here is a cat _____ a fish.

Directions: Find and circle the word **and**. It can go → or ↓.

a	n	d	e	b	r
i	t	a	n	d	e
k	l	a	n	e	x
e	z	n	a	n	b
m	o	d	a	d	c

How many did you circle? _____

Spectrum Sight Words
Grade K

Sight Word Vocabulary

9

Target words: is, a, and

Directions: Say each word as you trace it. Then, write each word on the line.

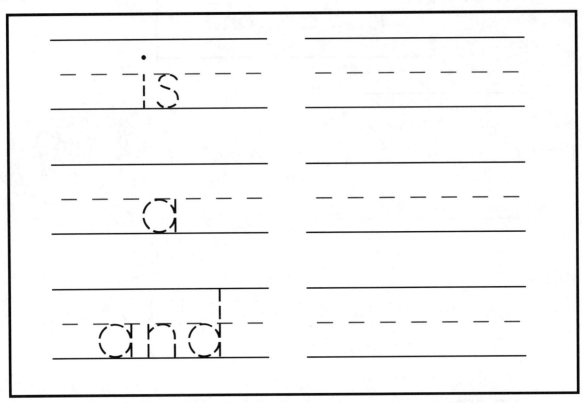

Directions: Draw lines to connect the words that match. Then, draw a dog bone by your favorite word.

Target words: see, we

Directions: Write the missing word in each sentence.

see	we

1. Do you _____ the monkey?

2. _____ can _____ the monkey.

3. I can _____ him swing.

Directions: Find and circle the word **see**. It can go → or ↓.

m	e	k	e	s	r
o	t	s	e	e	t
q	l	i	k	e	x
e	s	e	e	p	v
s	o	e	a	d	c

How many did you circle? _____

Target words: **we**

Directions: Color the spaces that have the same word as the one in the middle of the circle.

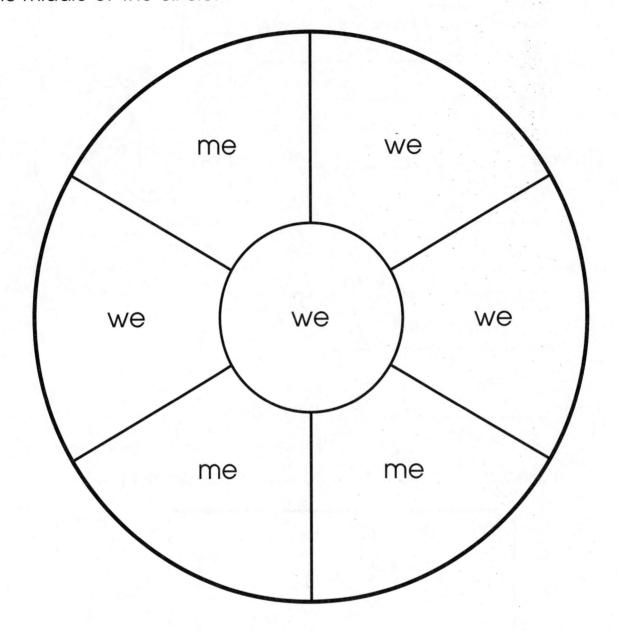

How many spaces did you color? _____

Target words: is, a, and, see, we

Directions: Find and circle the words **is**, **a**, **and**, **see**, and **we**. Words can go → or ↓.

i	s	e	e
s	s	k	s
w	s	n	b
x	a	w	w
a	n	d	e

Directions: Write the missing word in each sentence.

_____

— — — — — — —

1. I see _____ cat.

_____

— — — — — — —

2. I see a cat _____ a bee.

_____

— — — — — — — —

3. The cat can _____ a bee.

_____

— — — — — — —

4. The cat _____ happy.

_____

— — — — — —

5. _____ like the cat.

Target words: **have, us, our**

Directions: Say each word as you trace it. Then, write each word on the line.

Directions: Draw lines to connect the words that match. Then, draw a teddy bear face by your favorite words.

Target words: **have, us, our**

Directions: Draw lines to connect the words that rhyme.

us	sour
our	bus

Directions: Look for the words on the road. Circle them each time you see them.

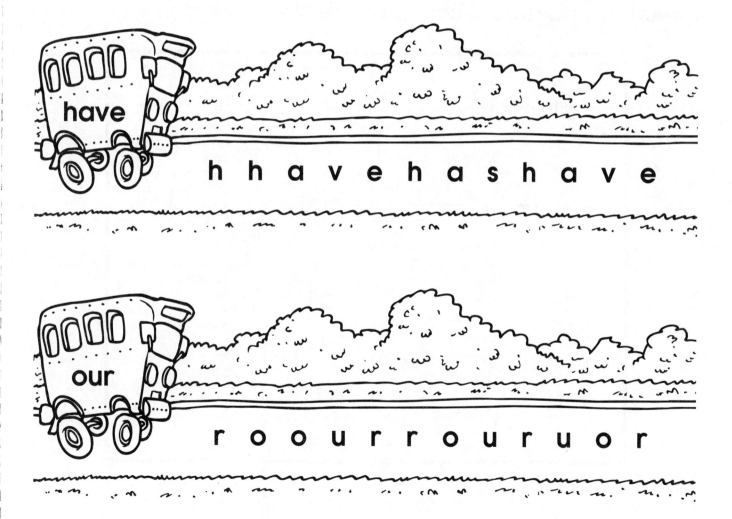

have

h h a v e h a s h a v e

our

r o o u r r o u r u o r

Target words: **it, all**

Directions: Say each word as you trace it. Then, write each word on the line.

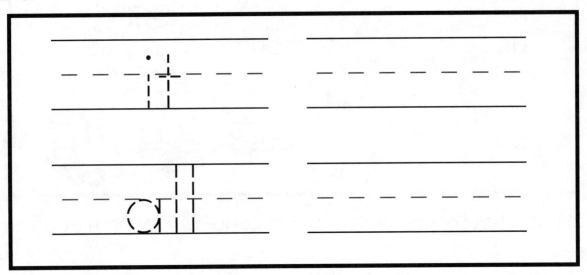

Directions: Draw lines to connect all the words that rhyme.

all   sit

ball

it   tall

hit

Target words: it

Directions: Color the spaces that have the same word as the one in the middle of the circle.

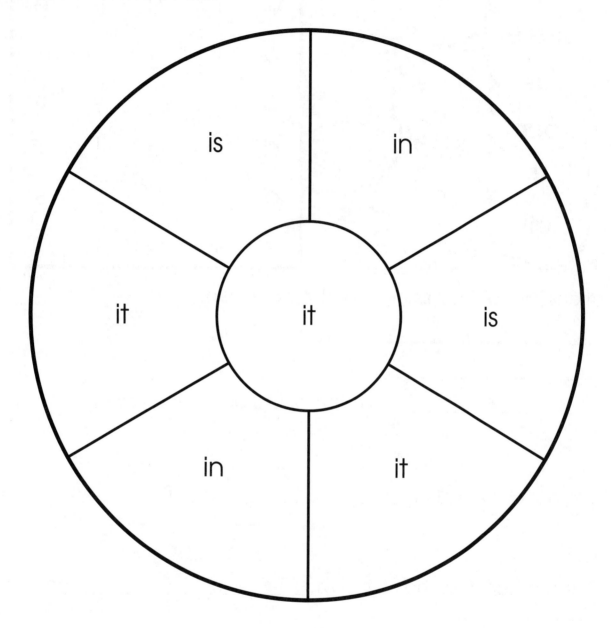

How many spaces did you color? _____

Target words: have, us, our, it, all

Directions: Find and circle the words in the box. Words can go →
or ↓.

w	h	a	v	e
p	u	s	m	l
a	t	l	y	s
d	o	a	l	l
d	u	u	r	s
i	r	q	i	t

Directions: Write the missing word in each sentence.

_____

– – – – – – –

1. _____ of the ducks are in the water.

_____

– – – – – – –

2. We have a pond on _____ farm.

_____

– – – – – – –

3. The mother duck has a baby. _____ can swim.

_____

– – – – – – – –

4. I _____ a toy duck.

_____

– – – – – – –

5. Will they play with _____ ?

Target words: **I, like, see, us, have**

Directions: Say each word as you write it on a circle. Color the circles blue.

I   like   see   us   have

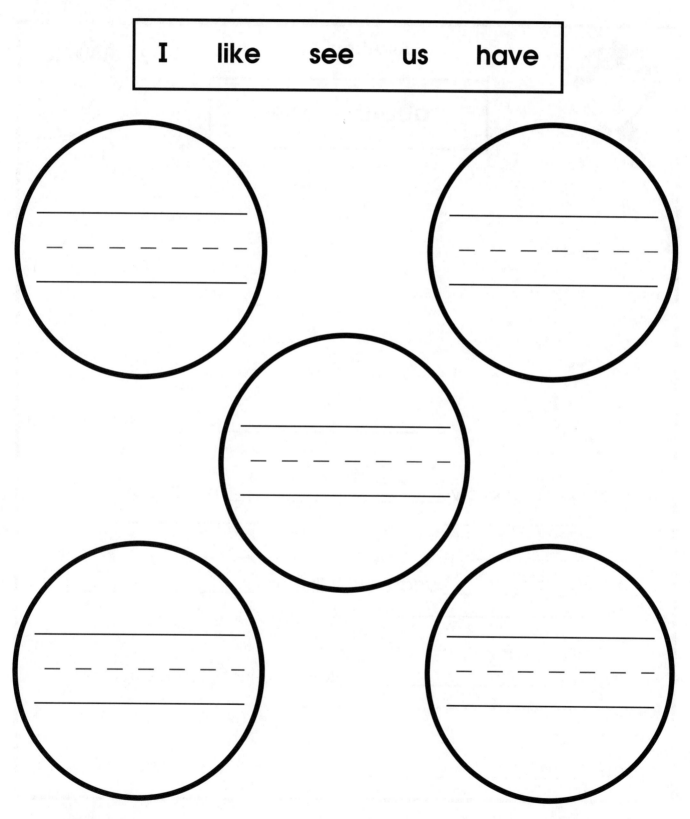

Target words: about, me

Directions: Draw a picture of yourself. Then, fill in the sentences to make a story.

All About Me

about	me

_____

– – – – – – –

Do you want to know _____ me? I am

_____   _____

– – – – – – –   – – – – – – –

_____ years old. I like to _____.

_____

– – – – – – –

I have a _____. Now you know some things

_____

– – – – – – –

about _____.

Target words: me

Directions: Color the spaces that have the same word as the one in the middle of the circle.

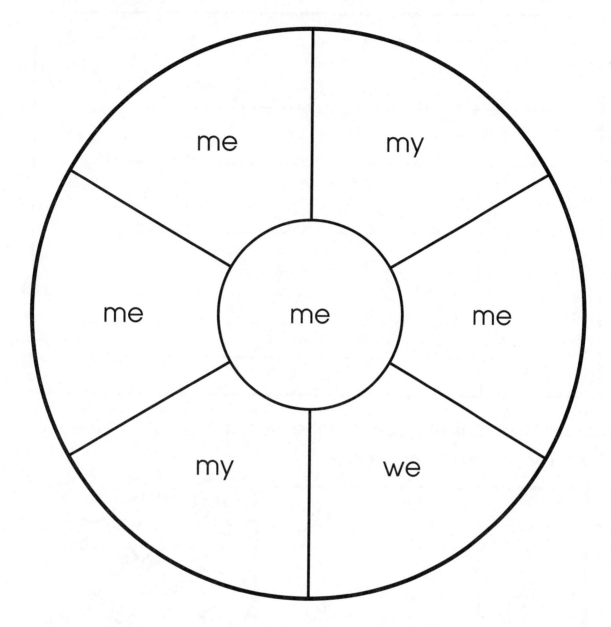

How many spaces did you color? _____

Target words: **no, this, do**

Directions: Say each word as you trace it. Then, write each word on the line.

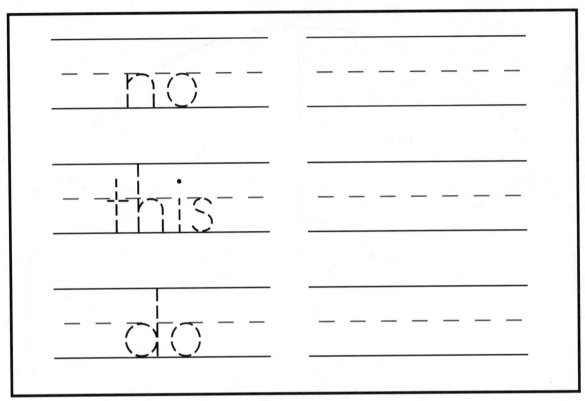

Directions: Draw lines to connect the words that match. Then, put a cat face by your favorite words.

Target words: no, this, do

Directions: Write the missing word in each sentence. Use the words in the box.

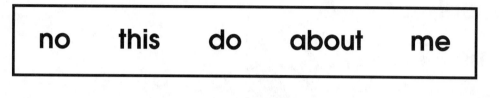

no	this	do	about	me

_____

– – – – – – – – –

1. Do you know _____ mice and elephants?

_____

– – – – – – – – –

2. _____ you like the mouse?

_____

– – – – – – – – –

3. _____, I do not like the mouse.

_____   _____

– – – – – – –   – – – – – – –

4. _____ mouse does not like _____.

Directions: Follow the words across the elephant tracks. Write them in a sentence.

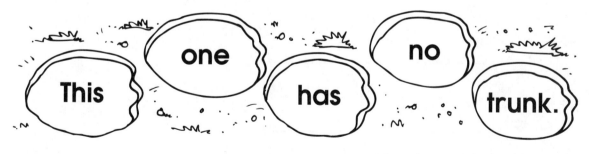

_____

– – – – – – – – – – – – – – – – – – – –

_____

Target words: about, me, no, this, do

Directions: Find and circle the words in the box. Words can go →
or ↓.

t	h	i	s	f
s	t	m	e	o
a	b	o	u	t
n	o	t	h	i
u	m	y	d	l
b	o	r	o	e

Directions: Write the missing word in each sentence.

_____
_ _ _ _ _ _ _

1. I know _____ turtles.

_____
_ _ _ _ _ _ _

2. _____ you know about turtles?

_____
_ _ _ _ _ _ _

3. _____ turtle is happy.

_____
_ _ _ _ _ _ _

4. Will it bite _____?

_____
_ _ _ _ _ _ _

5. _____, it will not bite you!

Target words: go, up, down

Directions: Say each word as you trace it. Then, write each word on the line.

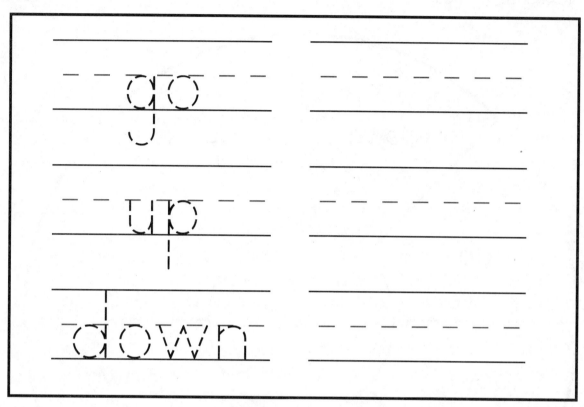

Directions: Turtle needs your help. Draw lines to connect the words that start with the same sound. Then, draw a turtle by your favorite words.

Target words: **down**

Directions: Color the spaces that have the same word as the one in the middle of the circle.

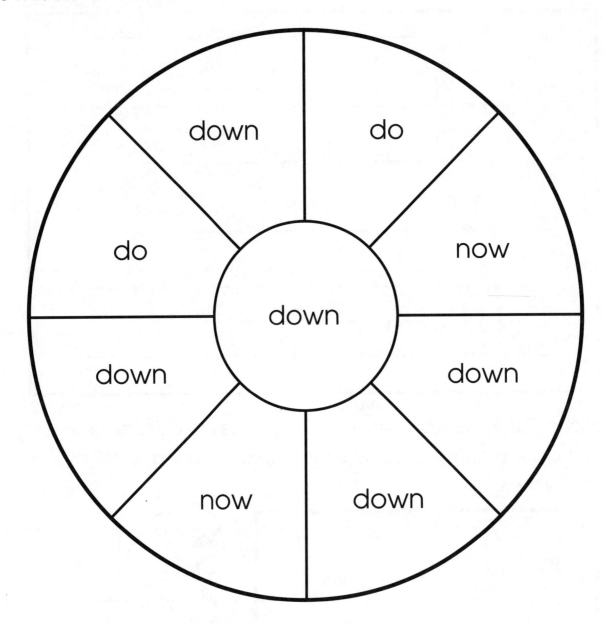

How many spaces did you color? _____

Target words: **who, has**

Directions: Say each word as you trace it. Then, write each word on the line.

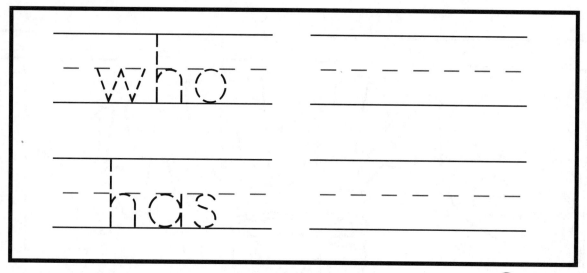

Directions: Read this sentence aloud. Then, write it on the line: **Who has the stick?**

_____

– –

_____

Directions: Color the boxes that have the words **who** and **has** in them:

who	have	we	has
has	we	who	have
who	has	we	has
have	who	has	who

Target words: **who, has**

Directions: Read the words in the box. Find and circle the birthday cakes that have the words **who** and **has** on them.

How many cakes did you circle? _____

Target words: go, up, down, has, who

Directions: Read each
sentence aloud. Then, write
each sentence on the lines.

Cars go down the hill.

_____

- - - - - - - - - - - - - - - - - - - -

_____

I see a car go up.

_____

- - - - - - - - - - - - - - - - - - - -

_____

Who has the best car?

_____

- - - - - - - - - - - - - - - - - - - -

_____

Is a red car here?

_____

- - - - - - - - - - - - - - - - - - - -

_____

This is our car.

_____

- - - - - - - - - - - - - - - - - - - -

_____

Target words: all, about, me, and, this

Directions: Read the words in the box. Then, write each word on a cake. Color the candles to show how old you are.

all	about	me	and	this

Target words: **are, put**

Directions: Say each word as you trace it. Then, write each word on the line.

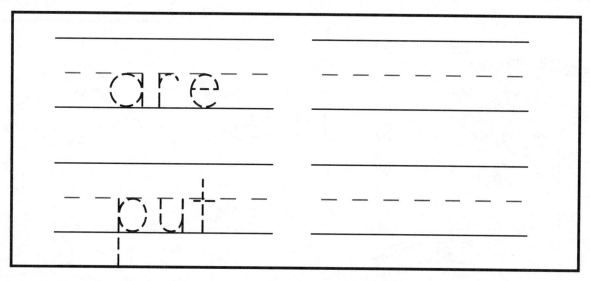

Directions: Circle the two words in each row that are the same.

put	put	pet	pat
out	our	out	over
are	at	art	are
and	an	am	and

Directions: Say the words as you write this question:
Where did you put the car?

_____

– – – – – – – – – – – – – – – – – –

_____

Target words: are, put

Directions: Help the monkey find the bananas with **are** and **put**. Circle those bananas.

are   put

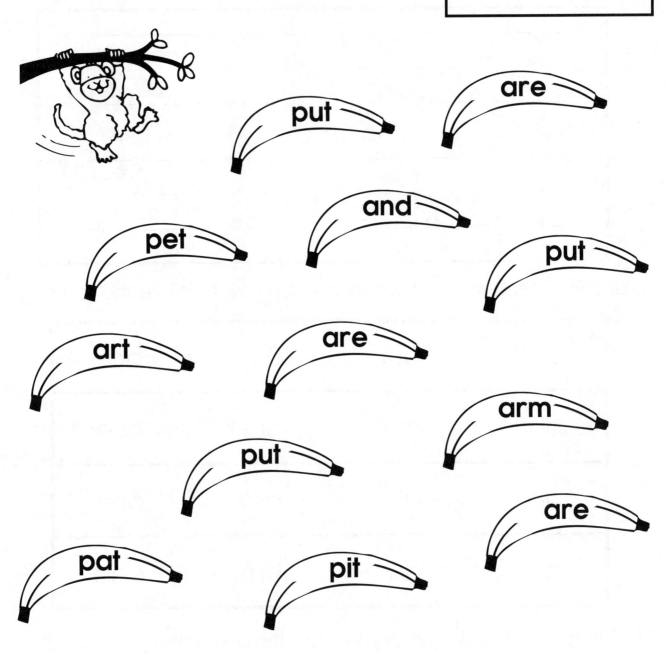

How many bananas did you circle? _____

Target words: in, on, out

Directions: Say each word as you trace it. Then, write each word on the line.

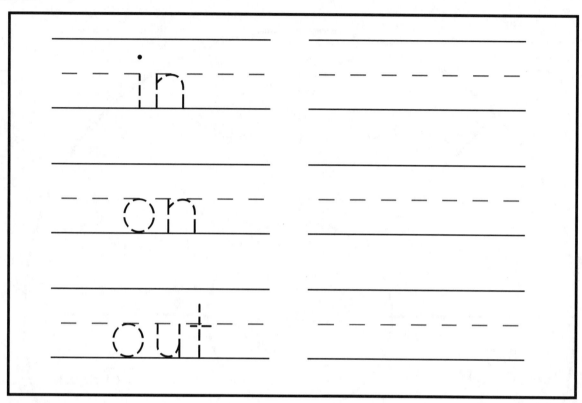

Directions: Find and circle the fish that have **in**, **on**, and **out** on them.

in	on	out

How many fish did you circle? _____

Target words: **on**

Directions: Color the spaces that have the same word as the one in the middle of the circle.

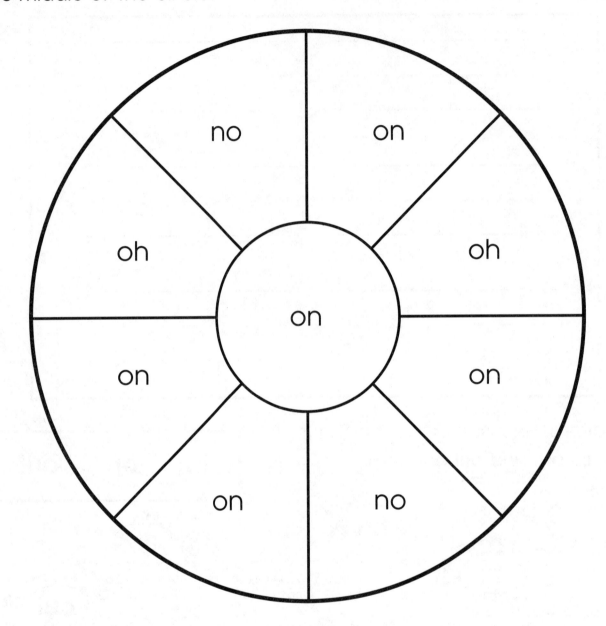

How many spaces did you color? _____

Target words: are, put, in, on, out, this

Directions: Say each word as you write it on a line. Then, color the pumpkins orange.

| are | put | in | on | out | this |

_____

- - - - - - - - - - -

_____

_____

- - - - - - - - - - -

_____

_____

- - - - - - - - - - -

_____

_____

- - - - - - - - - - -

_____

_____

- - - - - - - - - - -

_____

_____

- - - - - - - - - - -

_____

Target words: **by, can**

Directions: Say each word as you trace it. Then, write each word on the line.

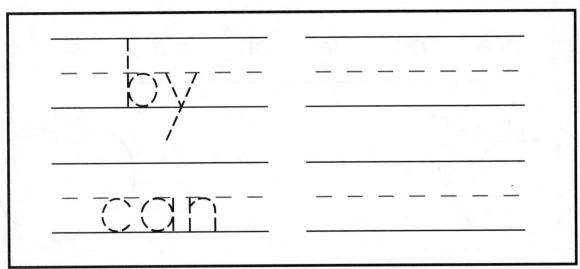

Directions: Write the missing word in each sentence. Then, say the words as you write the whole sentence.

by	can

I _____ see a bird.

_____

It is sitting _____ the tree.

_____

Target words: by, can

Directions: Find and circle the apples that have **by** and **can** on them.

How many apples did you circle? _____

Target words: what, you, make

Directions: Write the words from the box on the lines.

what	you	make

_____ _____ _____

- - - - - - - - - - - - - - - - - - - - - - -

_____ _____ _____

Directions: The word **what** is hiding in the rows below. It can go →
or ↓. Find and circle it.

```
t  h  a  t  h  h  e  t
w  h  a  t  h  e  a  e
h  t  a  w  a  h  t  w
a  w  h  a  t  w  a  h
w  h  e  a  h  t  w  a
h  a  w  h  a  t  h  t
```

Target words: **what**

Directions: Color the spaces that have the same word as the one in the middle of the circle.

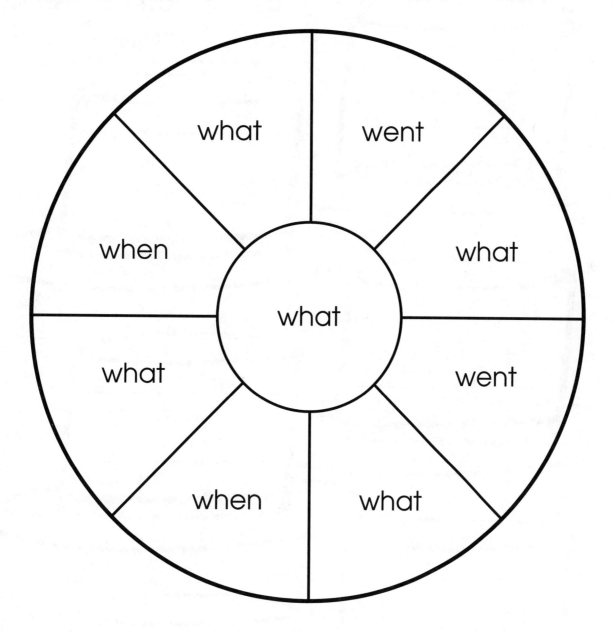

How many spaces did you color? _____

Target words: by, can, what, you, make, put

Directions: Write each word from the box on a line.

by	can	what
you	make	put

Target words: an, good

Directions: Write each word from the box on a line.

an   good

_____   _____

— — — — — — — —   — — — — — — — —

_____   _____

Directions: The word **good** is hiding below. It can go ➔ or ↓. Find and circle it.

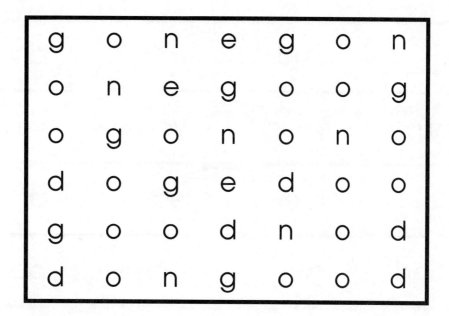

How many times did you find it? _____

Target words: an, good

Directions: Say each word as you trace it. Then, write each word on the line.

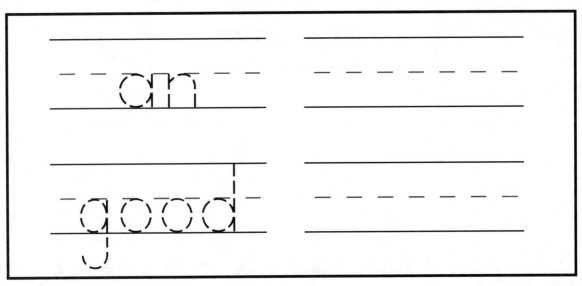

Directions: Circle the two words in each row that are the same.

an	and	am	an
you	your	you	yes
at	ate	eat	at
good	give	gone	good

Directions: Say the words as you write this question:

Can you make a pie that is good?

_____

_ _ _ _ _ _ _ _ _ _ _ _ _ _ _ _ _ _ _ _

_____

Target words: at, eat, get

Directions: Say each word as you trace it. Then, write each word on the line.

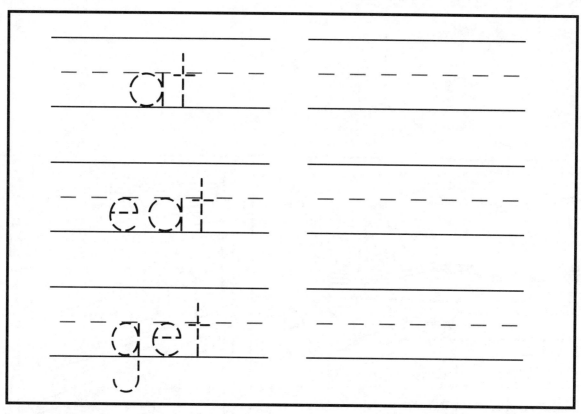

Directions: Color the boxes that have **at**, **eat**, and **get** in them. Use a different color for each word.

get	an	at	go
gone	ate	the	get
ate	eat	got	and
at	get	eat	at

Target words: at, eat, get

Directions: Say the word **eat** as you trace it. Then, write it on the line.
Circle the foods that you like to eat.

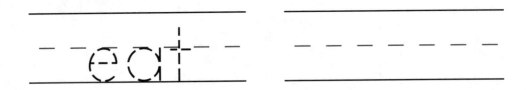

Which is your favorite food? Write a sentence about it. Then, read
your sentence aloud.

_____

I like _____.

Target words: an, good, at, eat, get

Directions: Find and circle the words in the box. Words can go →
or ↓.

an

good

at

eat

get

j	e	t	y	m	s
x	a	n	a	t	q
g	g	o	o	d	w
e	a	t	g	o	m
t	t	z	e	t	a
q	o	i	u	h	e

Directions: Write the missing word in each sentence.

_____

– – – – – –

1. The pig is _____ the food bin.

_____

– – – – – – –

2. The pig will _____ the food.

_____

– – – – – – –

3. Is the food _____?

_____

– – – – – – –

4. The pig will _____ a good snack.

_____

– – – – – – – –

5. The pig will make _____ oink when he is full!

Target words: **can, at, you, make, get**

Directions: Say each word as you write it on a line. Then circle the word that rhymes with **hat**.

at	can	get	make	you

_____

- - - - - - - - - - - - - - -

_____

_____

- - - - - - - - - - - - - - -

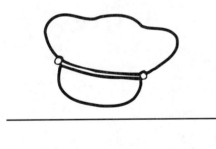

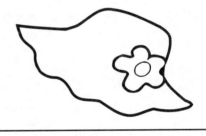

_____

- - - - - - - - - - - - - - -

_____

Directions: Fill in the missing word.

_____

- - - - - - - - - - - - - - -

Can _____ make a hat?

Target words: give, from

Directions: Find and circle the hearts that have **give** and **from** on them.

How many did you circle?   give _____   from _____

Target words: give, from

Directions: Say each word as you trace it. Then, write each word on the line.

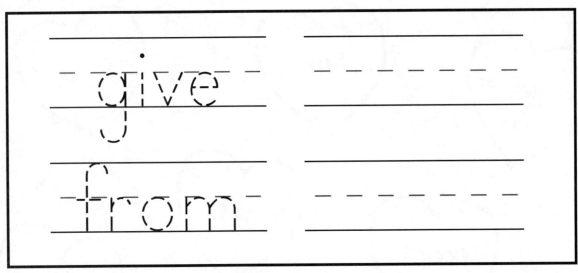

Directions: Circle the two words in each row that are the same.

can	cat	car	can
from	four	from	for
ate	eat	at	ate
give	good	gone	give

Directions: Say the words as you write this sentence:

Give him the note from me.

Dear Jack,
I will see you
after school.
Love, Mom

_____

- -

_____

Target words: they, boy, girl, he

Directions: Write the missing word in each sentence.

they	boy	girl	he

_____
_ _ _ _ _ _ _

1. A _____ named Ted lives in the house.

_____   _____
_ _ _ _ _ _ _ .   _ _ _ _ _ _ _

2. _____ has a sister. She is a _____.

_____
_ _ _ _ _ _ _

3. _____ like to play outside in the yard.

Directions: Draw a picture of the boy and girl playing in the yard.

Target words: they

Directions: Color the spaces that have the same word as the one in the middle of the circle.

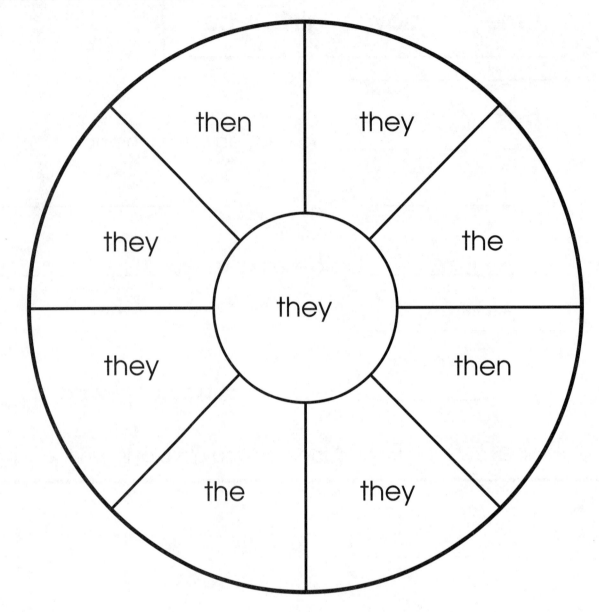

then they they the they they the then

How many spaces did you color? _____

Directions: Finish this sentence.

_____

— — — — — — — —

_____ like to run.

Target words: give, from, they, boy, girl, he

Directions: Find and circle the words in the box. Words can go →
or ↓.

give
from
they
boy
girl
he

b	y	u	b	h	y
g	i	r	l	e	n
i	f	b	o	y	m
v	r	a	b	o	t
e	o	t	h	e	y
f	m	c	a	n	e

Directions: Write the missing word in each sentence.

_____

– – – – – – – –

1. _____ is a shaggy dog.

_____   _____

– – – – – – –   – – – – – –

2. He belongs to a _____ and a _____.

_____

– – – – – – –

3. _____ like the dog.

_____

– – – – – – – –

4. The dog will get a good snack _____ the boy.

_____

– – – – – – –

5. The girl will _____ the dog a hug.

Spectrum Sight Words
Grade K

Sight Word Vocabulary

Target words: she, then

Directions: Find and circle the sheep that have the words **she** and **then** on them.

she	then

How many did you circle? _____

Sight Word Vocabulary

Target words: **then**

Directions: Color the spaces that have the same word as the one in the middle of the circle.

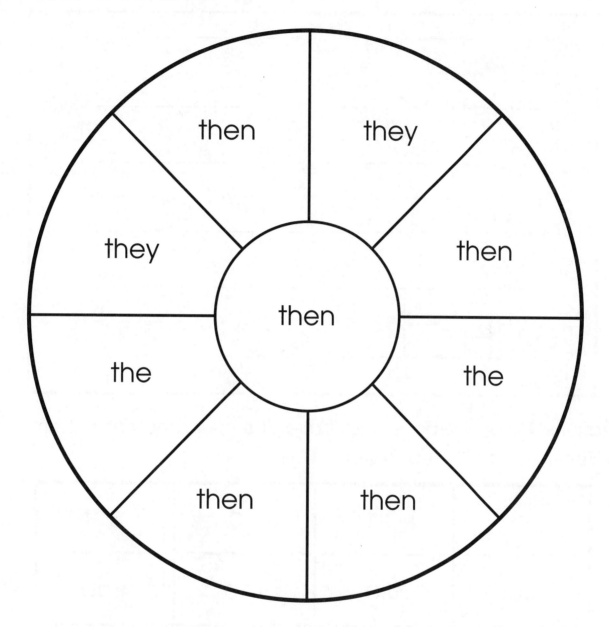

How many spaces did you color? _____

Target words: did, your, not

Directions: Say each word as you trace it. Then, write each word on the line.

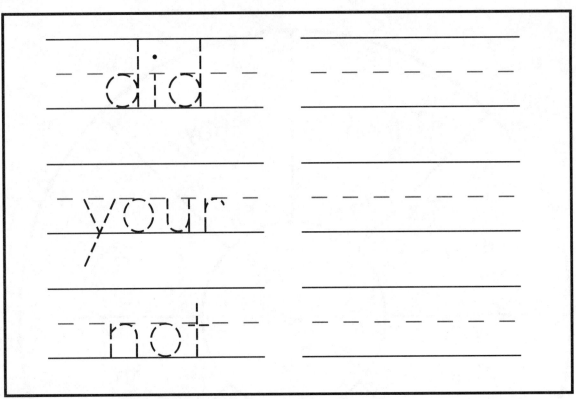

Directions: Color the boxes that have **did**, **your**, and **not** in them. Use a different color for each word.

you	on	no	not
your	did	the	you
do	not	got	no
did	no	your	did

Which word did you color the most? _____

Sight Word Vocabulary

Target words: did, your, not

Directions: Find and circle the ice cream cones with **did**, **your**, and **not** on them.

did	your	not

How many ice cream cones did you circle? _____

Target words: she, then, did, your, not

Directions: Find and circle the words in the box. Words can go →
or ↓.

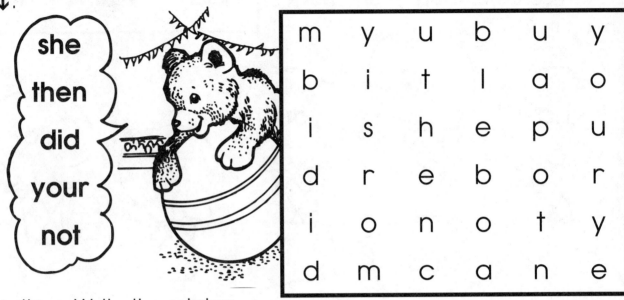

m	y	u	b	u	y
b	i	t	l	a	o
i	s	h	e	p	u
d	r	e	b	o	r
i	o	n	o	t	y
d	m	c	a	n	e

she
then
did
your
not

Directions: Write the missing
word in the sentence.

_____
— — — — — — —

1. Is that _____ bear?

_____
— — — — — —

2. _____ the bear take your ball?

_____
— — — — — — —

3. She did _____ take my ball.

_____
— — — — — — —

4. _____ where did she get it?

_____
— — — — — — —

5. _____ got the ball from the boy.

Target words: she, give, boy, they, eat

Directions: Say each word as you write it on a line.

she	they	give
eat	boy	

Directions: Fill in the missing word.

_____

She will give the _____ an apple to eat.

Target words: will, his

Directions: Say each word as you trace it. Then, write each word on the line.

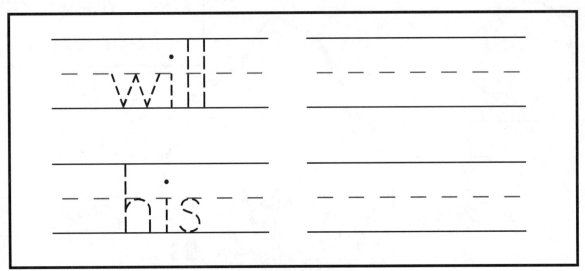

Directions: Circle the two words in each row that are the same.

they	the	they	than
his	is	his	him
when	will	we	will
was	saw	want	saw

Directions: Say the words as you write this sentence:
I will give the boy his toy.

_____

– –

_____

Target words: **his**

Directions: Color the spaces that have the same word as the one in the middle of the circle.

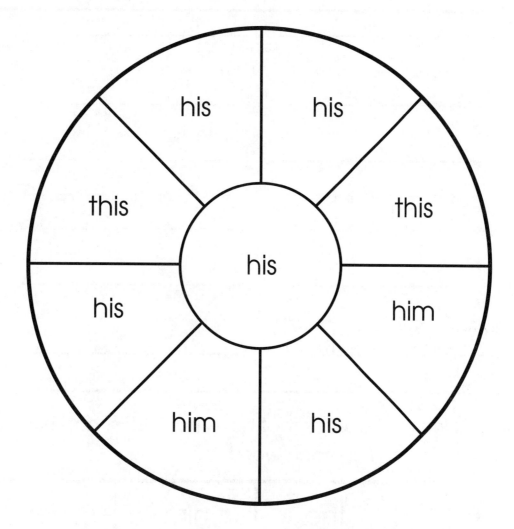

Directions: Write a sentence using the word in the middle of the circle.

_____

_ _ _ _ _ _ _ _ _ _ _ _ _

_____

_ _ _ _ _ _ _ _ _ _ _ _ _

_____

Target words: her, their, him

Directions: Say each word as you trace it. Then, write each word on the line.

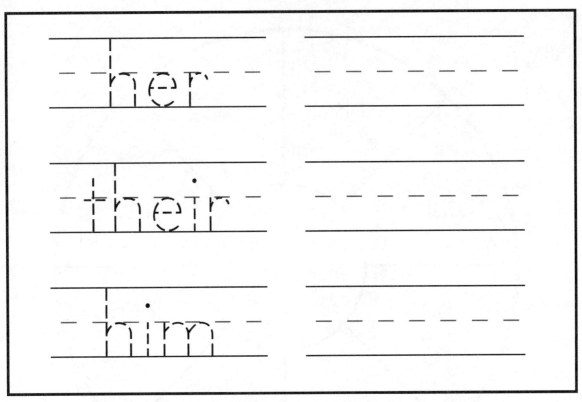

Directions: Color the squares that have **her**, **their**, and **him** in them. Use a different color for each word.

his	the	him	her
him	their	the	him
them	his	got	here
he	their	him	her

Which word did you color the most? _____

Target words: her, their, him

Directions: Find and circle the turtles that have the words **her**, **their**, and **him** on them.

| her | their | him |

How many turtles did you circle? _____

Target words: will, his, her, their, him

Directions: Find and circle the words in the box. Words can go →
or ↓.

m	h	u	b	u	y
b	i	t	l	a	o
i	s	h	e	r	u
d	w	i	l	l	r
i	o	m	o	t	y
d	t	h	e	i	r

will

his

her

their

him

Directions: Write the missing
word in each sentence.

_____

‗ ‒ ‒ ‒ ‒ ‒ ‒

1. The boy and girl have a bear. They like _____
    bear.

    _____

    ‗ ‒ ‒ ‒ ‒ ‒ ‒

2. _____ the bear let the balloon go?

    _____

    ‗ ‒ ‒ ‒ ‒ ‒ ‒

3. Did the girl give _____ balloon to the bear?

    _____

    ‗ ‒ ‒ ‒ ‒ ‒ ‒

4. No, the boy gave _____ balloon to the bear.

    _____

    ‗ ‒ ‒ ‒ ‒ ‒ ‒

5. Will the girl give _____ her balloon now?

Target words: them, know

Directions: Say each word as you trace it. Then, write each word on the line.

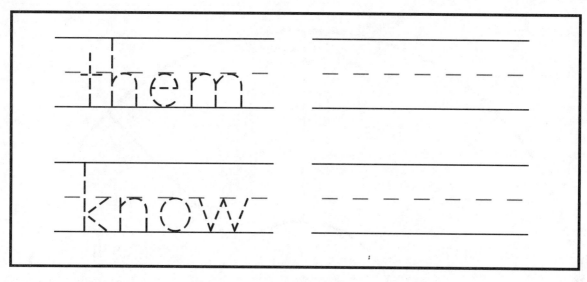

Directions: The words **them** and **know** are hiding in the lines below. Find and circle them.

Target words: **them**

Directions: Color the spaces that have the same word as the one in the middle of the circle.

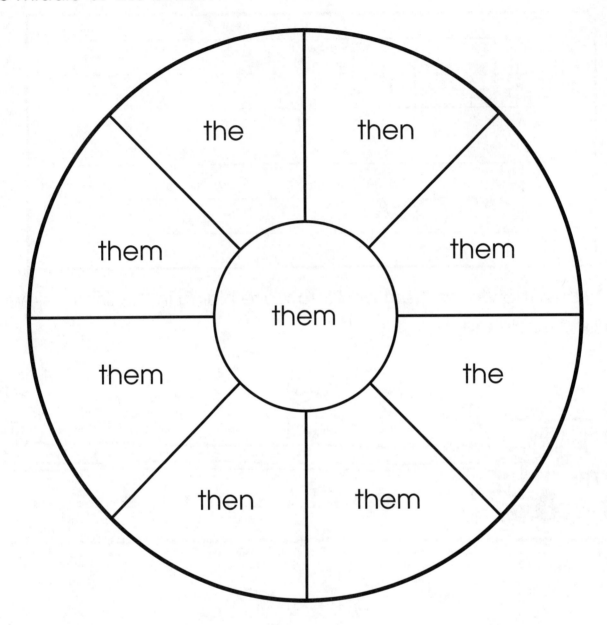

How many spaces did you color? _____

Sight Word Vocabulary

Target words: day, after, before

Directions: Find and circle the letters that have **day**, **after**, and **before** on them.

day   after   before

before

say

after

for

be

day

day

been

again

before

before

after

day

again

be

say

for

after

before

after

been

day

How many of each did you find?

day _____   after _____   before _____

Target words: day, after, before

Directions: Say each word as you trace it. Then, write each word on the line.

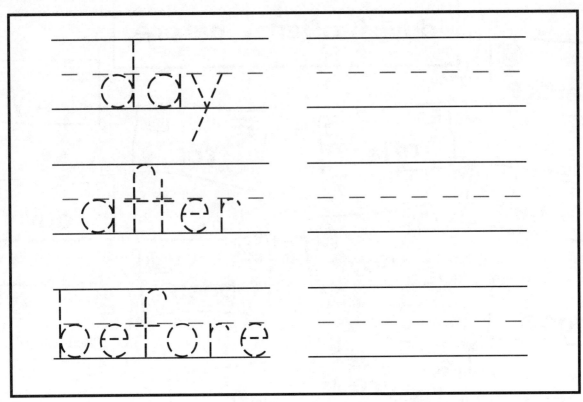

Directions: Circle the two words in each row that are the same.

day	date	day	dart
before	begin	been	before
after	ate	often	after
go	got	gone	go

Directions: Say the words as you write this sentence:

Go the day after today.

Sun.	Mon.	Tues.	Wed.	Thu.	Fri.	Sat.
1	2	3	4	5	6	7
8	9	10	11	12	13	14
15	16	17	18	19	20	21
22	23	24	25	26	27	28

Target words: them, know, day, after, before

Directions: Find and circle the words in the box. Words can go →
or ↓.

| them |
| know |
| day |
| after |
| before |

k	n	t	h	e	m
b	e	f	o	r	e
a	d	a	t	t	d
y	e	s	h	h	a
a	f	t	e	r	y
k	n	o	w	n	s

Directions: Write the missing
word in each sentence.

1. Do you _____ about penguins?

2. What do you know about _____?

3. _____ they swim, they jump in the water.

4. _____ they swim, they can rest.

5. It is a long _____ for them!

Target words: long, again, been

Directions: Say each word as you trace it. Then, write each word on the line.

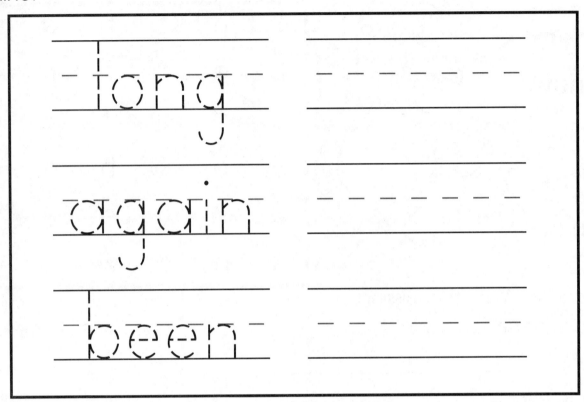

Directions: Color the boxes that have these words in them. Use a different color for each word.

long	again	been

before	like	long	again
long	again	the	been
long	after	rain	again
been	look	been	then

Target words: long, again, been

Directions: Find and circle the leaves with the words **long**, **again**, and **been** on them.

| long | again | been |

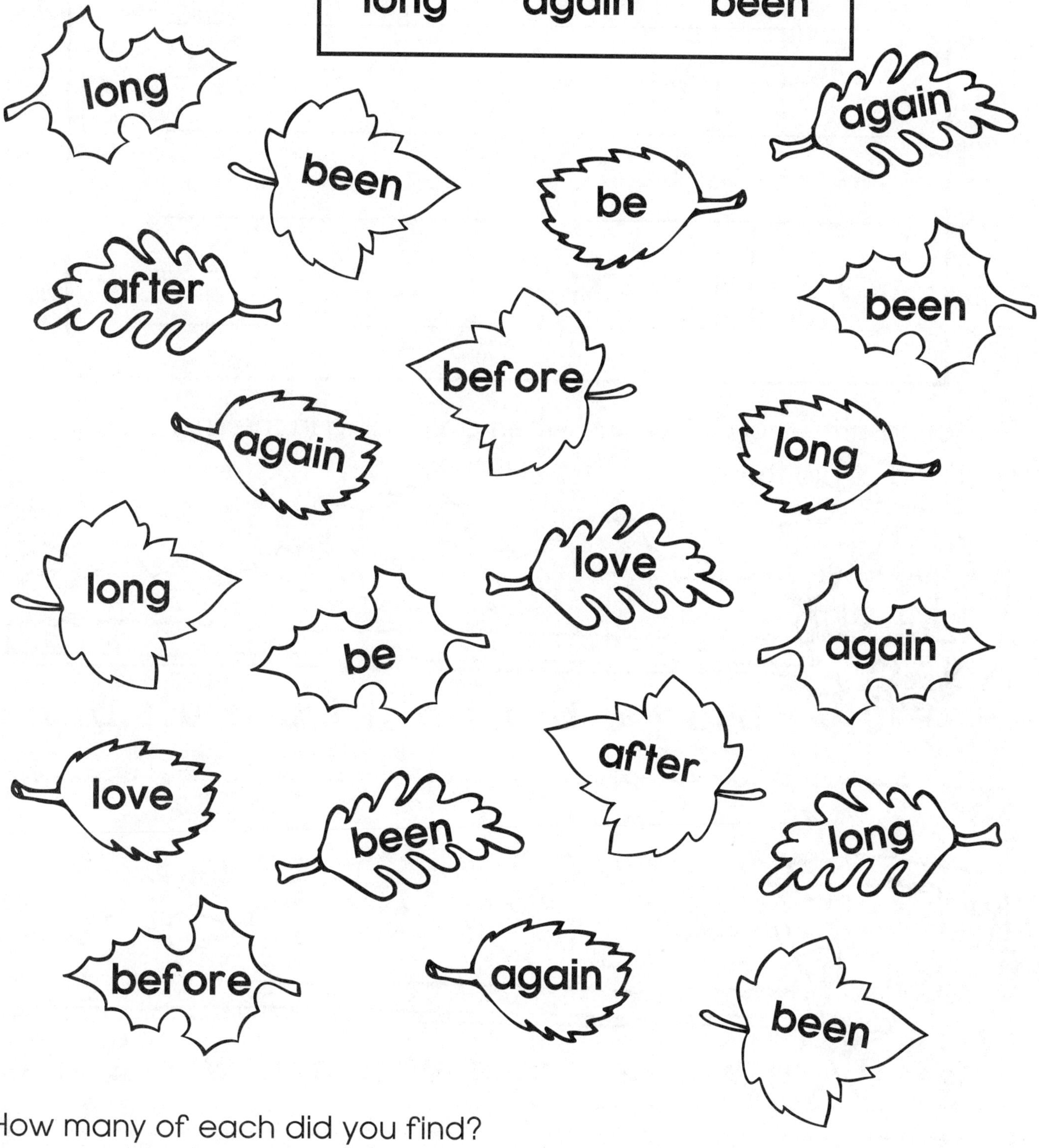

long

been

be

again

after

been

before

again

long

long

love

again

be

love

after

been

long

before

again

been

How many of each did you find?

long _____   again _____   been _____

Target words: but, when

Directions: Say each word as you trace it. Then, write each word on the line.

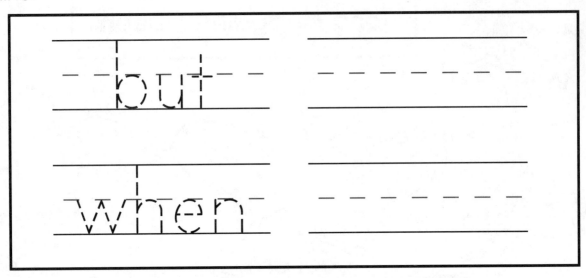

Directions: The words **but** and **when** are hiding in the lines below. Find and circle them.

How many did you find?   but _____   when _____

Target words: when

Directions: Color the spaces that have the same word as the one in the middle of the circle.

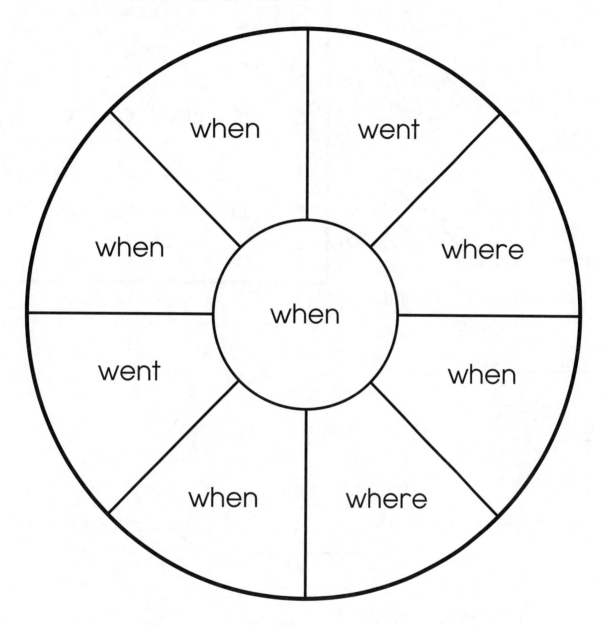

How many spaces did you color? _____

Target words: long, again, been, but, when

Directions: Find and circle the words in the box. Words can go →
or ↓.

long

again

been

but

when

a	b	u	t	u	y
g	e	r	l	a	n
a	e	b	o	y	m
i	n	l	o	n	g
n	o	t	h	e	y
f	m	w	h	e	n

Directions: Write the missing word in each sentence.

_____

– – – – – – –

1. _____ did the frog get here?

_____

– – – – – – – –

2. He hopped back here _____ after he left.

_____

– – – – – – – –

3. Where has he _____?

_____

– – – – – – – –

4. I do not know, _____ he was gone a

_____

– – – – – – – –

_____ time.

Target words: been, long, when, they, on

Directions: Say each word as you write it on a line.

been	long	when	they	on

_____

- - - - - - - - - - - - - - - -

_____

_____

- - - - - - - - - - - - - - - -

_____

- - - - - - - - - - - - - - - -

_____

_____

- - - - - - - - - - - - - - - -

_____

_____

- - - - - - - - - - - - - - - -

_____

Directions: Fill in the missing word:

_____

- - - - - - - - - - - -

They have been _____ a long ride.

Target words: day, after, before, the, is, on, go, to, know

Directions: Fill in the missing words. Use a calendar to help you.

Sunday	Monday	Tuesday	Wednesday	Thursday	Friday	Saturday
		1	2	3	4	5
6	7	8	9	10	11	12
13	14	15	16	17	18	19
20	21	22	23	24	25	26
27	28	29	30	31		

_____
_ _ _ _ _ _ _

1. Sunday is the day _____ Monday.

_____
_ _ _ _ _ _ _ _

2. Friday is the day _____ Thursday.

_____
_ _ _ _ _ _ _ _

3. On Monday I _____ to school.

_____   _____
_ _ _ _ _ _   _ _ _ _ _ _

4. I _____ there is no school _____ Saturday.

Target words: **was, my, very**

Directions: Find and circle the stars with the words **was**, **my**, and **very** on them.

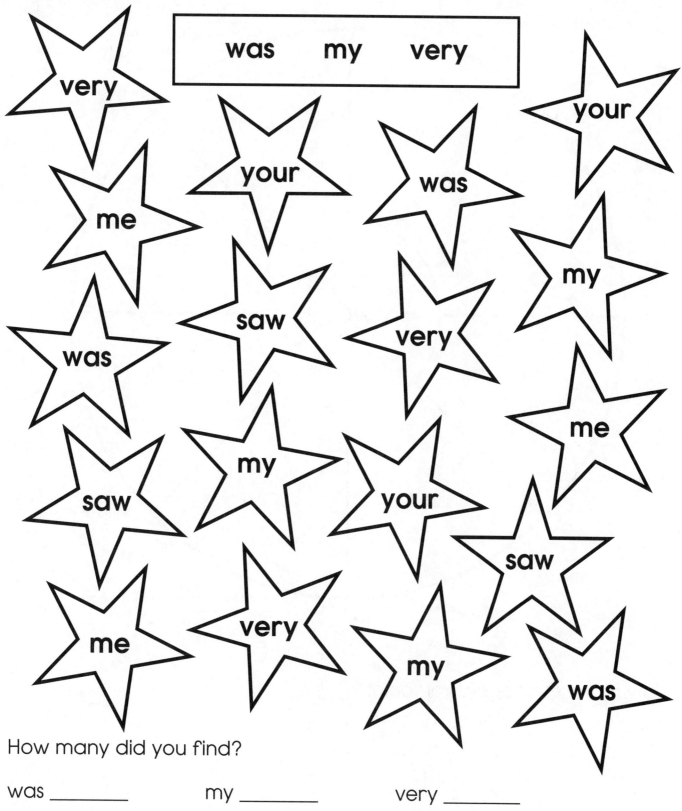

was   my   very

very

your

me

your

was

saw

was

very

my

saw

my

me

saw

your

me

very

saw

my

was

How many did you find?

was _____   my _____   very _____

Target words: **was**

Directions: Color the spaces that have the same word as the one in the middle of the circle.

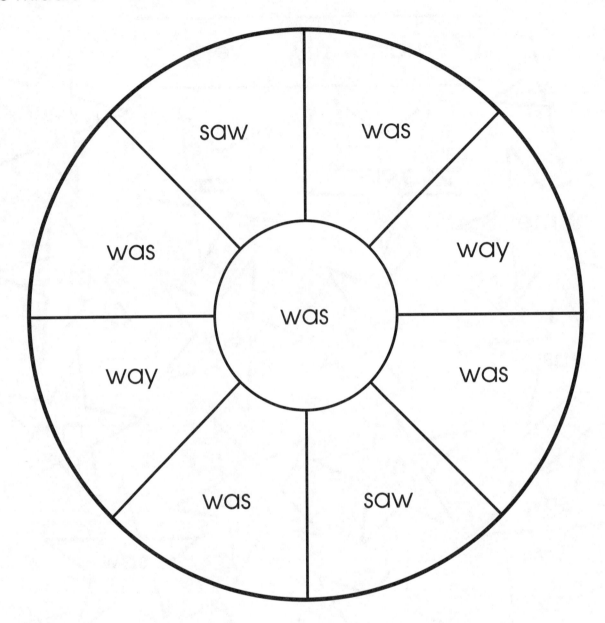

How many spaces did you color? _____

Target words: had, for, come

Directions: Say each word as you trace it. Then, write each word on the line.

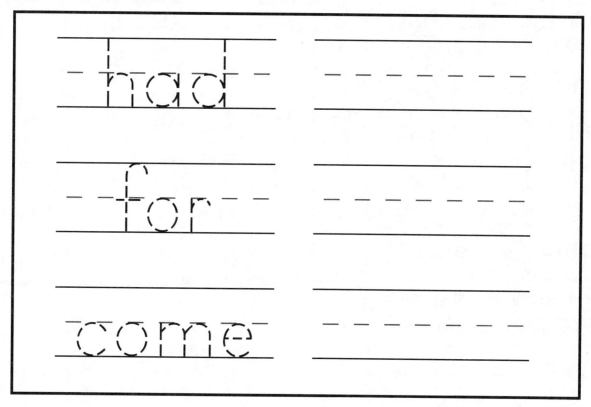

Directions: Color the boxes that have these words in them. Use a different color for each word.

had	for	come

come	for	some	had
had	come	had	have
long	after	from	some
for	come	has	for

Target words: was, my, very, had, for, come

Directions: Find and circle the words in the box. Words can go →
or ↓.

was
my
very
had
for
come

b	y	u	b	m	y
c	o	m	e	a	w
v	f	o	r	y	a
e	h	a	b	o	s
r	o	t	h	a	d
y	m	c	a	n	e

Directions: Write the missing
word in each sentence.

_____
_ _ _ _ _ _

1. This is _____ fish.

_____
_ _ _ _ _ _

2. He is my _____ favorite fish. He

_____
_ _ _ _ _ _

_____ little when I got him.

_____
_ _ _ _ _ _ _

3. When I feed him, he will _____ to the top of
   the tank.

Target words: **be, of, that**

Directions: Say each word as you trace it. Then, write each word on the line.

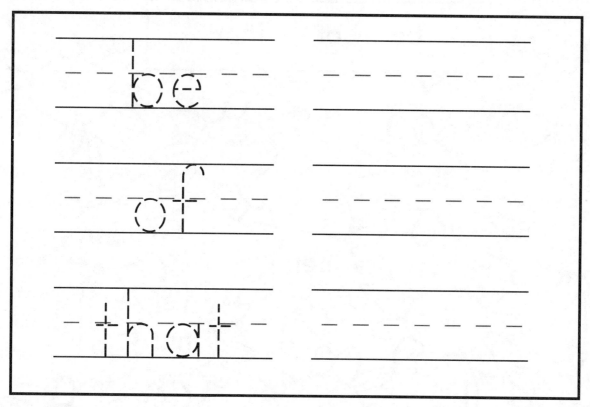

Directions: Circle the two words in each row that are the same.

been	be	but	be
if	on	of	of
at	that	that	ate
have	has	his	has

Directions: Say the words as you write this sentence:

It is king of the jungle.

- - - - - - - - - - - - - - - - - - - -

Target words: be, of, that

Directions: Find and circle the flowers with the words **be**, **of**, and **that** on them.

be   of   that

if

of

that

if

be

been

then

if

that

been

of

be

then

been

of

then

be

that

How many did you find?

be _____   of _____   that _____

Target words: **were, if, would**

Directions: Say each word as you trace it. Then, write each word on the line.

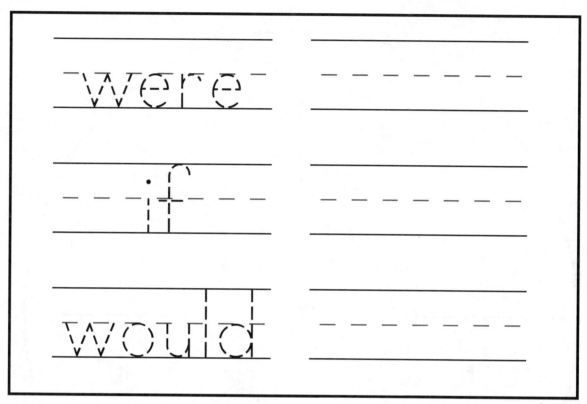

Directions: Color the boxes that have these words in them. Use a different color for each word.

	were	if	would	

was	for	would	if
if	for	of	have
long	would	from	where
of	were	has	for

How many did you find?

were _____   if _____   would _____

Target words: **if**

Directions: Color the spaces that have the same word as the one in the middle of the circle.

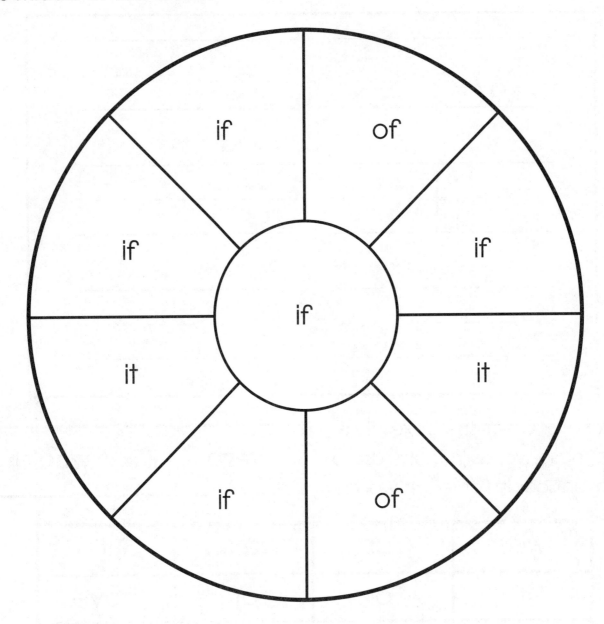

How many spaces did you color? _____

Target words: come, be, that, were, of

Directions: Say each word as you trace it. Then, write each word on the line.

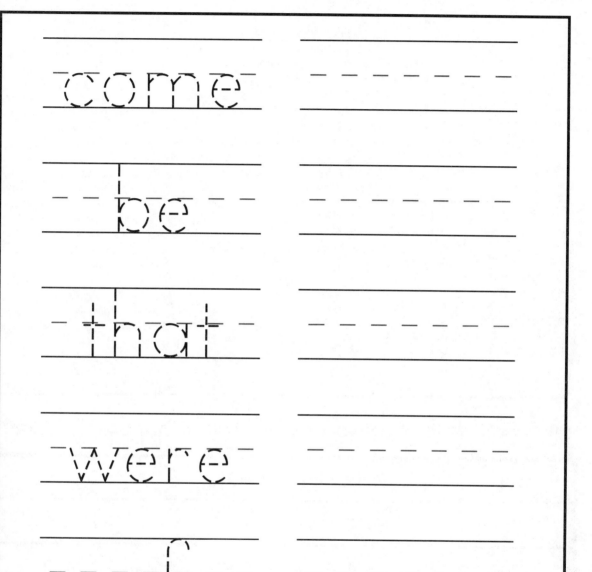

Target words: **just, there, so**

Directions: Say each word as you trace it. Then, write each word on the line.

Directions: Circle the two words in each row that are the same.

on	one	so	so
just	jeep	just	jump
then	there	the	there
was	were	went	were

Directions: Say the words as you write this sentence:

There are so many dogs!

_____

- - - - - - - - - - - - - - - - -

_____

Target words: just, there, so

Directions: Find and circle the pumpkins with the words **just**, **there**, and **so** on them.

just	there	so

How many did you find?

just _____   there _____   so _____

Target words: little, or, with

Directions: Say each word as you trace it. Then, write each word on the line.

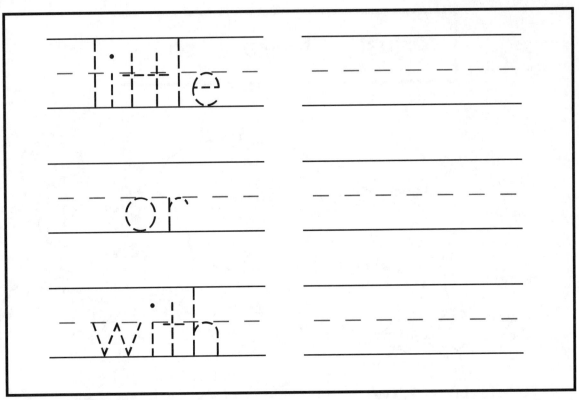

Directions: Help the duck find the words that start with the same letter. Draw a line to connect the words that match. Draw a baby duck by your favorite words.

little

with

or

old

bill

look

open

hike

were

Target words: **with**

Directions: Color the spaces that have the same word as the one in the middle of the circle.

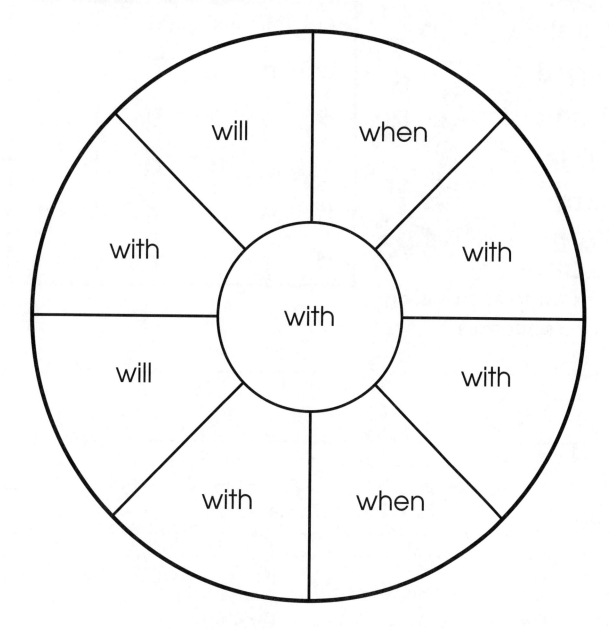

How many spaces did you color? _____

NAME _____

Target words: just, there, so, little, or, with

Directions: Find and circle the words in the box. Words can go →
or ↓.

q	t	r	e	l	x
w	h	g	u	i	j
i	e	j	u	t	u
t	r	s	o	t	s
h	e	t	r	l	t
d	j	o	r	e	n

Directions: Write each missing
word in the sentences.

_____   _____
_ _ _ _ _ _ _ _ _   _ _ _ _ _ _ _ _ _

1. _____ is a _____ mouse.

   _____
   _ _ _ _ _ _ _ _

2. Is he there _____ a piece of cheese?

   _____
   _ _ _ _ _ _ _

3. Is he brown _____ gray?

   _____
   _ _ _ _ _ _ _ _

4. Why is he _____ little?

   _____
   _ _ _ _ _ _ _

5. He is _____ a baby.

Sight Word Vocabulary

Target words: be, very, little, from, the, up

Directions: Say each word as you trace it. Then, write each word on the line.

Target words: **one, two, three**

Directions: Say each word as you trace it. Then, write each word on the line.

  one

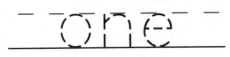

 two

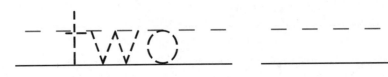

 three

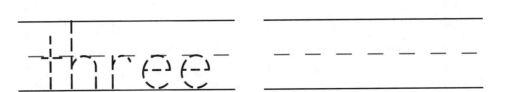

Directions: Draw a line to match the numbers to their words.

three	2
one	3
two	1

Draw a picture to show each number.

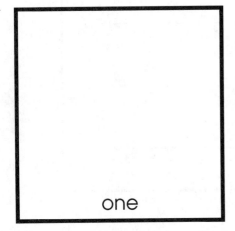

one

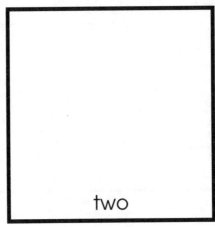

two

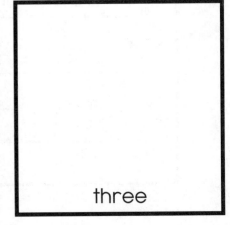

three

Target words: **one**

Directions: Color the spaces that have the same word as the one in the middle of the circle.

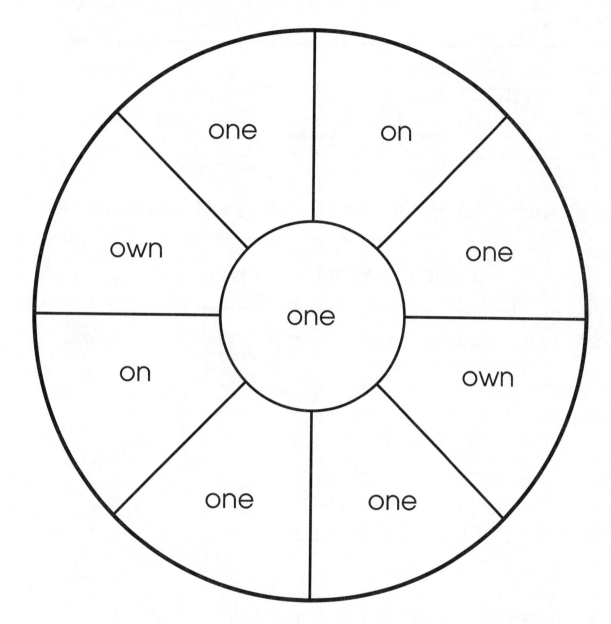

How many spaces did you color? _____

Target words: four, five, work

Directions: Write each number word under the correct number.

| 1 | 2 | 3 | 4 | 5 |

three

Directions: Use the words in the box to complete these sentences.

| four | work | five |

1. Start at two and jump three places ahead. Where did you

   stop? _____

2. This is hard _____ .

3. Start at five and jump back one space. Where did you

   stop? _____

Target words: one, two, three, four, five

Directions: Draw a line to connect the number words in order. Start with **one**.

| one | two | three | four | five |

Target words: one, two, three, four, five

Directions: Write the correct number word on each line.

one   two   three   four   five

1 _____

2 _____

3 _____

4 _____

5 _____

Target words: **how, old, as**

Directions: Say each word as you trace it. Then, write each word on the line.

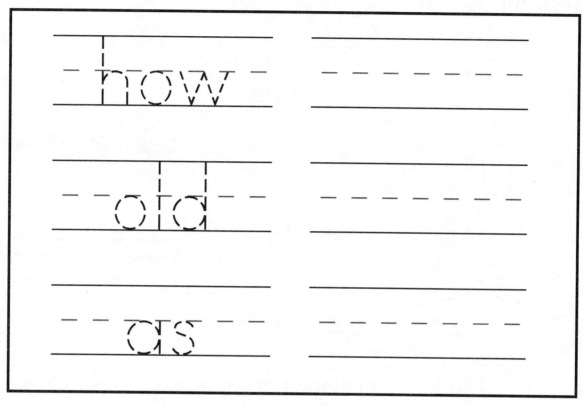

how

old

as

Directions: Draw a line to connect the words that rhyme. Then, draw a paw print by your favorite pair.

cold	has
now	old
as	how

Target words: how, old, as

Directions: Read and answer the questions below.

1. How old are you?

    _____

    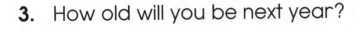

    I am _____ years old.

2. Draw candles on the cake to
    show how old you are.

3. How old will you be next year?

    _____

    — — — — — — — —

    I will be _____ years old.

4. Draw a picture of a present that you want for your birthday.

    [ ]

5. How tall will you be?

    _____

    — — — — — — — — —

    I will be as tall as a _____.

Target words: said, take, some

Directions: Say each word as you trace it. Then, write each word on the line.

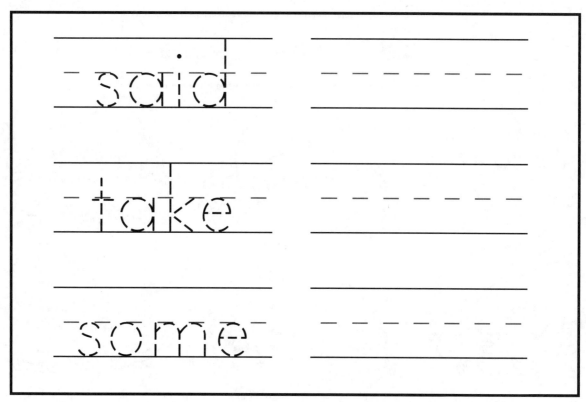

Directions: Color the boxes that have these words in them. Use a different color for each word.

said	take	some

take	then	said	some
so	take	the	she
the	two	take	that
said	some	said	some

Target words: said, take, some

Directions: Find and circle the eggs with the words **said**, **take**, and **some** on them.

said	take	some

How many eggs did you circle?

said _____   take _____   some _____

Target words: how, old, as, said, take, some

Directions: Find and circle the words in the box. Words can go →
or ↓.

how
old
as
said
take
some

b	s	o	m	e	a
g	i	r	l	a	s
a	t	h	o	w	m
s	a	i	d	o	e
e	k	o	l	d	y
f	e	c	a	n	e

Directions: Write the missing
word in the sentence.

_____

‾ ‾ ‾ ‾ ‾ ‾ ‾ ‾

1. Do you want _____ eggs?

_____

‾ ‾ ‾ ‾ ‾ ‾ ‾ ‾

2. _____ many do you want to take?

_____

‾ ‾ ‾ ‾ ‾ ‾ ‾

3. The hen _____, "Cluck, cluck, cluck."

_____

‾ ‾ ‾ ‾ ‾ ‾ ‾ ‾

4. She does not want you to _____ her eggs.

Target words: other, any, much

Directions: Say each word as you trace it. Then, write each word on the line.

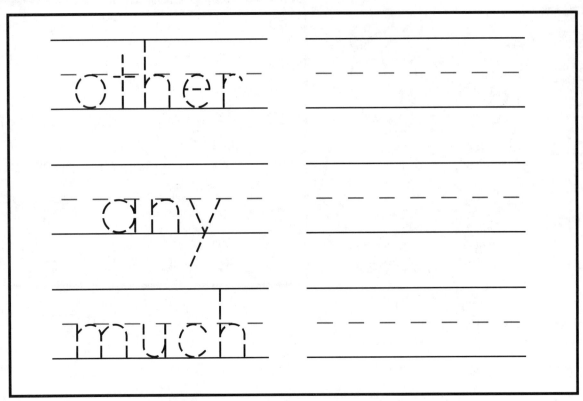

Directions: Draw a line to connect the words that rhyme.

other   many

any   such

much   mother

Target words: **any**

Directions: Color the spaces that have the same word as the one in the middle of the circle.

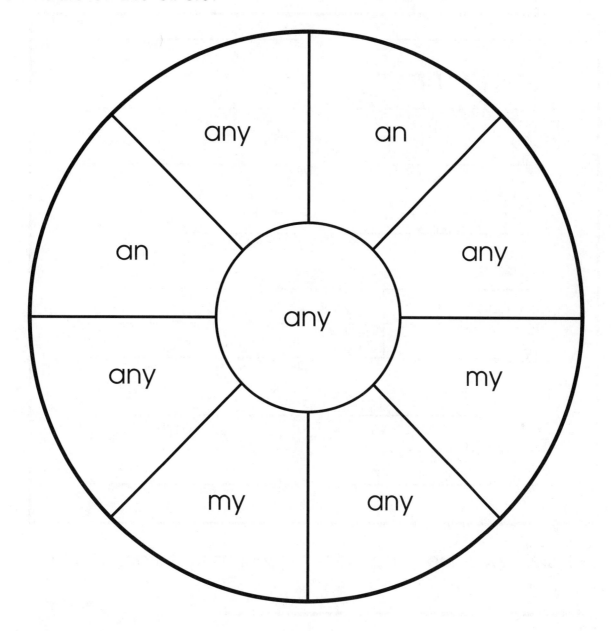

How many times did you find the word **any**? _____

What other words did you find? _____

Target words: **many, new, which, man**

Directions: Say each word as you trace it. Then, write each word on the line.

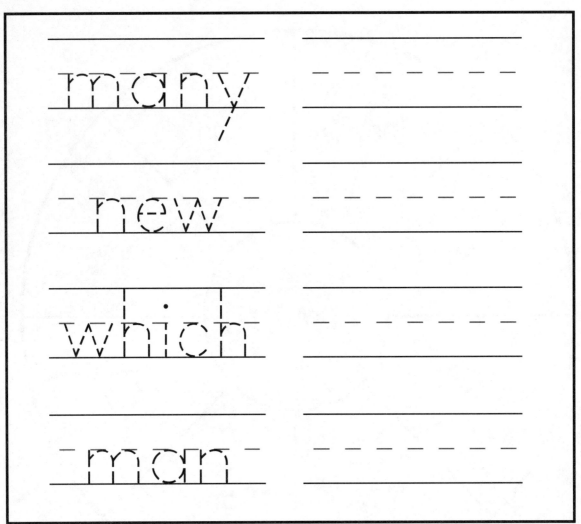

Directions: Draw a line to connect the words that start with the same sound.

which	me
new	make
man	not
many	when

Target words: many, new, which, man

Directions: Find and circle the mittens with the words from the box on them.

many	new	which	man

munch

new

any

much

many

when

some

man

much

was

which

any

munch

new

many

was

which

some

man

when

Target words: many, which, much, other, man

Directions: Read the words in the box. Then, write the words under the flowers.

many	which	much	other	man

_ _ _ _ _ _ _ _ _ _

_ _ _ _ _ _ _ _ _ _

_ _ _ _ _ _ _ _ _ _

_ _ _ _ _ _ _ _ _ _

_ _ _ _ _ _ _ _ _ _

Sight Word Sentence Strips

Sight word sentence strips provide additional practice recognizing and using sight words in the context of sentences, a critical first step in reading comprehension and fluency. The sight words used in the following sentence strips appear in the order they were introduced.

The sentence strips can be used in a number of ways, depending on each child's developmental level. Begin by encouraging your child to read each sentence strip aloud with the goal of fluent sight word recognition, offering praise for spontaneous recognition. Revisit the tracing activities for those sight words that still need additional practice, and evaluate progress by having your child locate those words from among the sight word flash cards.

Help your child develop sentence sense by helping him or her notice the characteristics of the first and last words in each sentence, such as the capitalized first word and the ending punctuation following the last word. Then, ask if the sentence would still make sense if those words were in a different order. Finally, point out the specific order of the words in the "middle." Ask your child to say the words aloud in a different order to see if the sentence would still make sense.

For a more challenging activity, encourage your child to write a single sentence strip on a separate sheet of paper, cutting it into individual words. Then, using the sentence strip in the workbook as a model, ask your child to rearrange the cut-apart words into the correct sentence order. Remind him or her to pay attention to the capitalized word and the word with ending punctuation. Provide lots of encouragement and praise as your child recognizes the sight words in context of these sentences and begins to demonstrate an understanding of sentence sense.

I want to play.

We see the cat.

The car can go.

Do you like dogs?

Can he go up?

She plays with us.

The pig can eat.

A boy lives here.

She did not go.

I know about it.

It is for him.

Where is he?

This is my fish.

I see that girl.

There are so many!

Would you come?

He is not little.

There are five cats.

Do you have dogs?

How old are you?

We will take that.

I have a new toy.

Which book is that?

Sight Word Tracing

The words below are intended for extra practice in writing the sight words. They can be used for independent work, as a review, or for remediation. Some additional ways to use the words include the following:

- For individual assessment, say the sight words and have the child trace the words in different colors.

- For extended small-group practice after tracing the words, have children cut apart and alphabetize the words.

- For extended independent work after tracing the words, have children locate the words in books.

Directions: Say each word as you trace it. Then spell the word aloud.

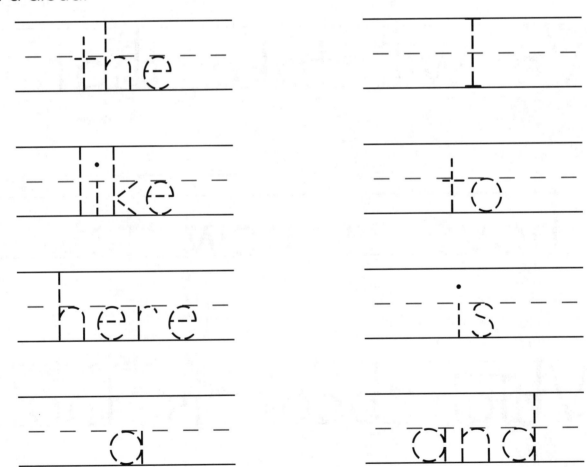

Tracing

see

we

have

us

our

it

all

about

me

no

this

do

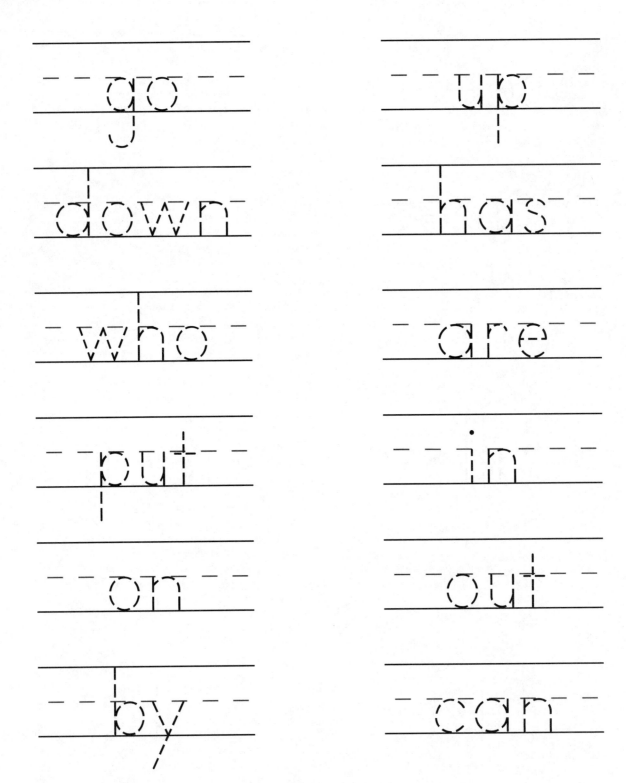

go

up

down

has

who

are

put

in

on

out

by

can

what

make

good

eat

give

they

you

an

at

get

from

boy

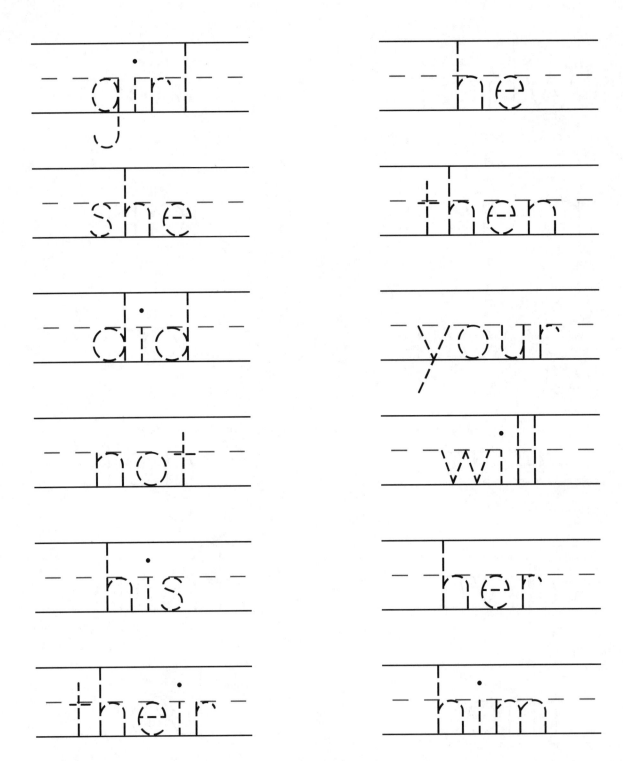

girl

she

did

not

his

their

he

then

your

will

her

him

them

day

before

again

but

was

know

after

long

been

when

my

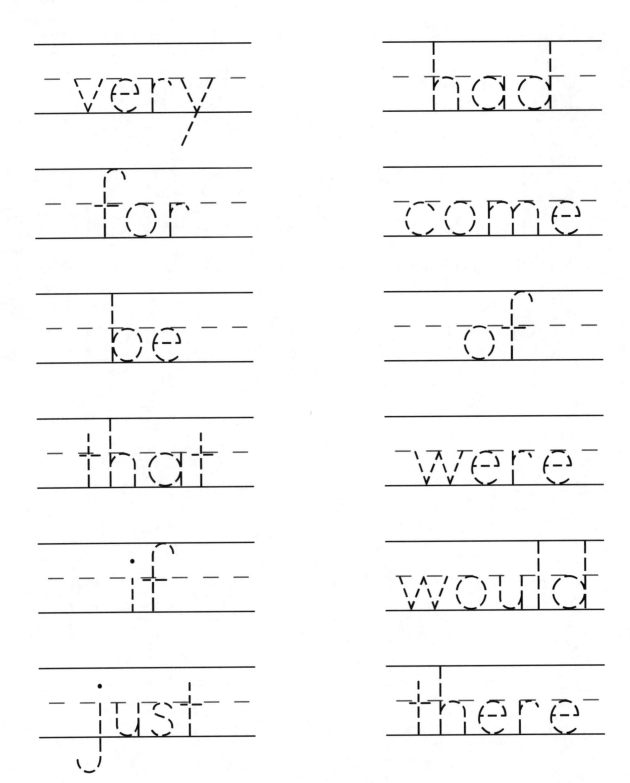

very

for

be

that

if

just

had

come

of

were

would

there

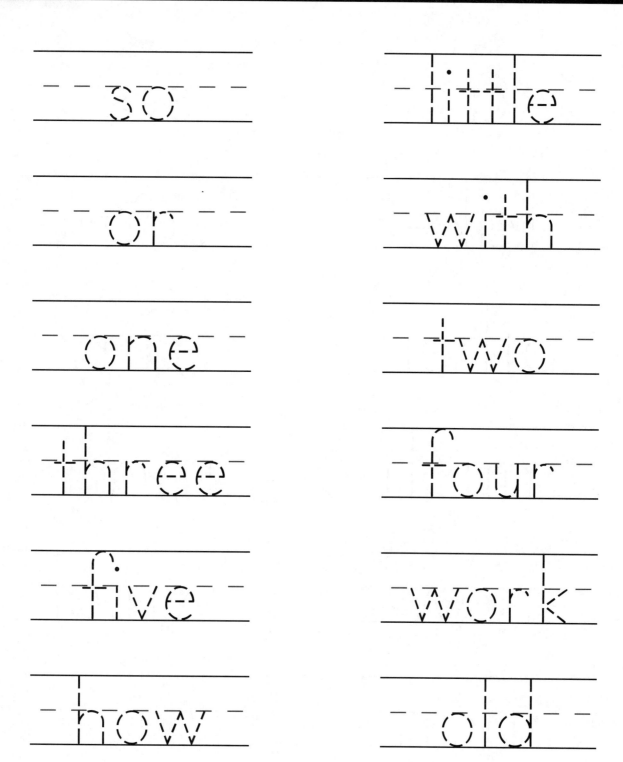

so

little

or

with

one

two

three

four

five

work

how

old

as

said

take

some

other

any

much

many

new

which

man

Sight Word Flash Cards

On the following pages are flash cards for all of the sight words used in this book. For ease of use, they are presented in the order of introduction in the book. Laminating the cards would also help make them durable. Punching a hole in each card and keeping them on a ring for each child is also a good way to keep the cards organized and easy to use.

There are many ways to use these cards. Listed below are some games and activities to help children learn to recognize the sight words:

- Sort the cards by sight words with the same beginning letter.

- Find sight words that rhyme, and write other words that rhyme with the sight words on a dry erase board or separate sheet of paper.

- Sort the cards to make pairs of sight words that begin with the same letter. Play the "Memory" game using these words—players don't get to keep the pair unless they can read both words. As an extension of this, also have players use the words in sentences.

- Use a timer to see how quickly each sight word is recognized. Begin with a small number of cards. Add more cards once increased speed and confidence is achieved.

- Put the sight words in alphabetical order.

- Come up with another word that begins with the same sound as each sight word.

the	I
like	to
here	is
a	and

see	we
have	us
our	it
all	about

me	no
this	do
go	up
down	has

who	are
put	in
on	out
by	can

what	you
make	an
good	at
eat	get

give	from
they	boy
girl	he
she	then

did	your
not	will
his	her
their	him

them	know
day	after
before	long
again	been

but	when
was	my
very	had
for	come

be	of
that	were
if	would
just	there

so	little
or	with
one	two
three	four

five	work
how	old
as	said
take	some

other	any
much	many
new	which
man	

Flash Cards

Fry Instant Sight Word List

First One Hundred Words

a	can	her	many	see	us
about	come	here	me	she	very
after	day	him	much	so	was
again	did	his	my	some	we
all	do	how	new	take	were
an	down	I	no	that	what
and	eat	if	not	the	when
any	for	in	of	their	which
are	from	is	old	them	who
as	get	it	on	then	will
at	give	just	one	there	with
be	go	know	or	they	work
been	good	like	other	this	would
before	had	little	our	three	you
boy	has	long	out	to	your
but	have	make	put	two	
by	he	man	said	up	

Fry Instant Sight Word List

Second One Hundred Words

also	color	home	must	red	think
am	could	house	name	right	too
another	dear	into	near	run	tree
away	each	kind	never	saw	under
back	ear	last	next	say	until
ball	end	leave	night	school	upon
because	far	left	only	seem	use
best	find	let	open	shall	want
better	first	live	over	should	way
big	five	look	own	soon	where
black	found	made	people	stand	while
book	four	may	play	such	white
both	friend	men	please	sure	wish
box	girl	more	present	tell	why
bring	got	morning	pretty	than	year
call	hand	most	ran	these	
came	high	mother	read	thing	

Fry Instant Sight Word List

Third One Hundred Words

along	didn't	food	keep	sat	though
always	does	full	letter	second	today
anything	dog	funny	longer	set	took
around	don't	gave	love	seven	town
ask	door	goes	might	show	try
ate	dress	green	money	sing	turn
bed	early	grow	myself	sister	walk
brown	eight	hat	now	sit	warm
buy	every	happy	o'clock	six	wash
car	eyes	hard	off	sleep	water
carry	face	head	once	small	woman
clean	fall	hear	order	start	write
close	fast	help	pair	stop	yellow
clothes	fat	hold	part	ten	yes
coat	fine	hope	ride	thank	yesterday
cold	fire	hot	round	third	
cut	fly	jump	same	those	

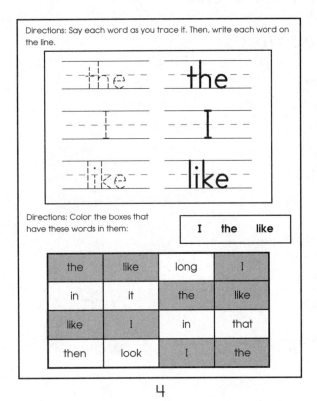

Directions: Say each word as you trace it. Then, write each word on the line.

the   the

I   I

like   like

Directions: Color the boxes that have these words in them:

I	the	like

the	like	long	I
in	it	the	like
like	I	in	that
then	look	I	the

4

Directions: Write the missing word in each sentence.

I	the	like

1. __I__ want to play.

2. Do you __like__ dogs?

3. Where is __the__ cat?

Directions: Find and circle the word **like**. It can go → or ↓.

l	i	k	e	b	r
i	t	l	i	k	e
k	l	i	k	e	x
e	z	k	w	p	v
m	o	e	a	d	c

How many did you circle? __5__

5

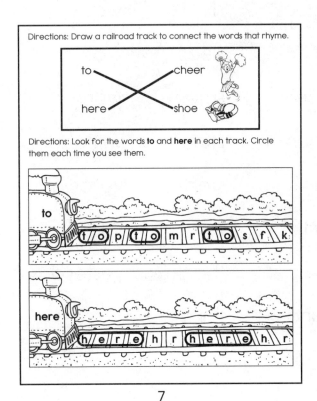

Directions: Draw a railroad track to connect the words that rhyme.

to   cheer

here   shoe

Directions: Look for the words **to** and **here** in each track. Circle them each time you see them.

to   t o p t o m r t o s f k

here   h e r e h r h e r e h r

7

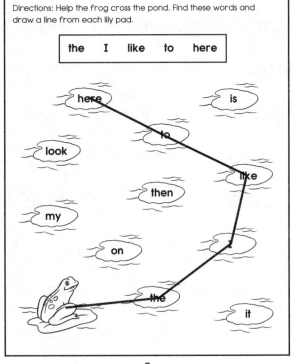

Directions: Help the frog cross the pond. Find these words and draw a line from each lily pad.

the	I	like	to	here

here   is

look   to

         like

      then

my

   on

      the   it

8

Answer Key

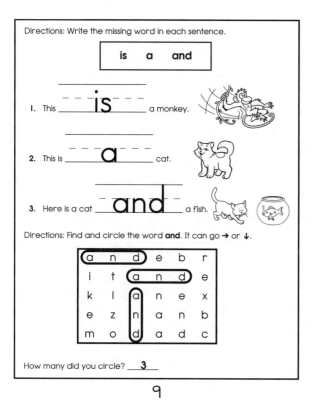

Directions: Write the missing word in each sentence.

| is | a | and |

1. This ___**is**___ a monkey.

2. This is ___**a**___ cat.

3. Here is a cat ___**and**___ a fish.

Directions: Find and circle the word **and**. It can go → or ↓.

a	n	d	e	b	r
i	t	a	n	d	e
k	l	a	n	e	x
e	z	n	a	n	b
m	o	d	a	d	c

How many did you circle? __**3**__

9

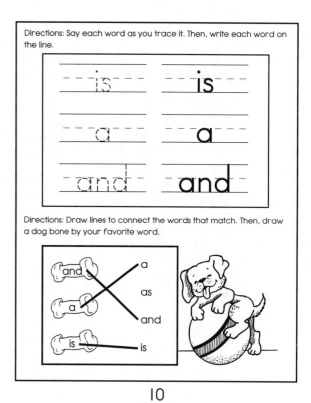

Directions: Say each word as you trace it. Then, write each word on the line.

is   is

a   a

and   and

Directions: Draw lines to connect the words that match. Then, draw a dog bone by your favorite word.

and   a
a   as
is   and
    is

10

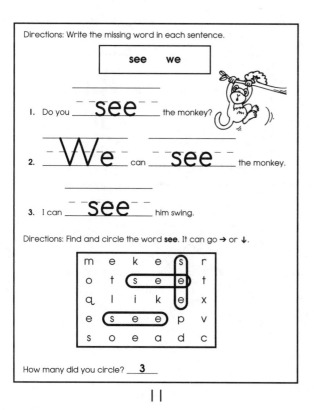

Directions: Write the missing word in each sentence.

| see | we |

1. Do you ___**see**___ the monkey?

2. ___**We**___ can ___**see**___ the monkey.

3. I can ___**see**___ him swing.

Directions: Find and circle the word **see**. It can go → or ↓.

m	e	k	e	s	r
o	t	s	e	e	t
q	l	i	k	e	x
e	s	e	e	p	v
s	o	e	a	d	c

How many did you circle? __**3**__

11

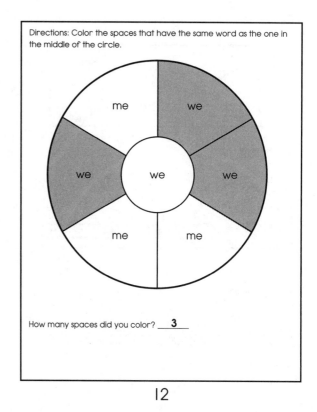

Directions: Color the spaces that have the same word as the one in the middle of the circle.

me   we
we   we   we
me   me

How many spaces did you color? __**3**__

12

Spectrum Sight Words
Grade K

Answer Key

139

Directions: Find and circle the words **is**, **a**, **and**, **see**, and **we**. Words can go → or ↓.

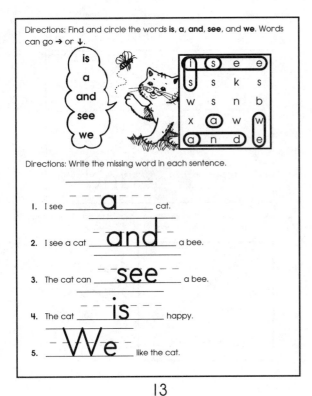

Directions: Write the missing word in each sentence.

1. I see _____ **a** _____ cat.

2. I see a cat _____ **and** _____ a bee.

3. The cat can _____ **see** _____ a bee.

4. The cat _____ **is** _____ happy.

5. **We** _____ like the cat.

13

Directions: Say each word as you trace it. Then, write each word on the line.

have   have
us   us
our   our

Directions: Draw lines to connect the words that match. Then, draw a teddy bear face by your favorite words.

have   is
        us
our   has
        your
us   have
        our

14

Directions: Draw lines to connect the words that rhyme.

us   sour
our   bus

Directions: Look for the words on the road. Circle them each time you see them.

have

h (have) has (have)

our

r o (our) r (our) u o r

15

Directions: Say each word as you trace it. Then, write each word on the line.

it   it
all   all

Directions: Draw lines to connect all the words that rhyme.

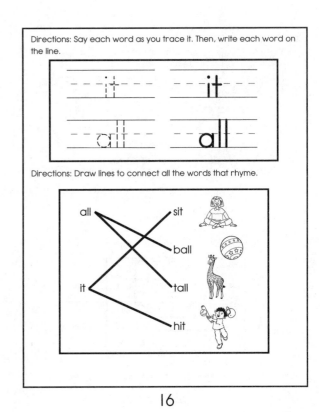

all   sit
            ball
it   tall
            hit

16

Directions: Color the spaces that have the same word as the one in the middle of the circle.

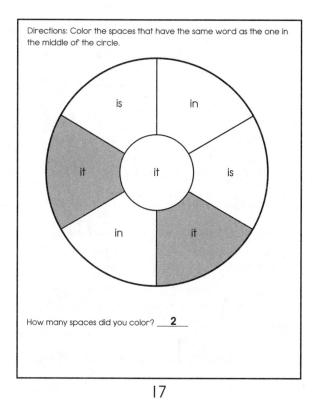

How many spaces did you color? __2__

17

Directions: Find and circle the words in the box. Words can go → or ↓.

have
us
our
it
all

w	h	a	v	e
p	u	s	m	l
a	t	l	y	s
d	o	a	l	l
d	u	u	r	s
i	r	q	i	t

Directions: Write the missing word in each sentence.

1. __All__ of the ducks are in the water.

2. We have a pond on __our__ farm.

3. The mother duck has a baby. __It__ can swim.

4. I __have__ a toy duck.

5. Will they play with __us__ ?

18

Directions: Draw a picture of yourself. Then, fill in the sentences to make a story.

All About Me

about   me

Pictures will vary.

Do you want to know __about__ me? I am

Answers will vary.

I have a _____. Now you know some things

about __me__ .

20

Directions: Color the spaces that have the same word as the one in the middle of the circle.

How many spaces did you color? __3__

21

Spectrum Sight Words
Grade K

Directions: Say each word as you trace it. Then, write each word on the line.

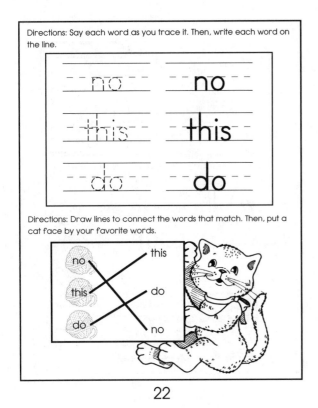

no   no

this   this

do   do

Directions: Draw lines to connect the words that match. Then, put a cat face by your favorite words.

Directions: Write the missing word in each sentence. Use the words in the box.

| no | this | do | about | me |

1. Do you know **about** mice and elephants?

2. **Do** you like the mouse?

3. **No**, I do not like the mouse.

4. **This** mouse does not like **me**.

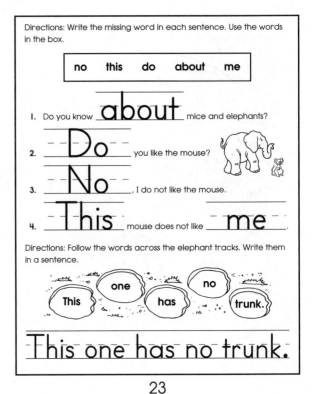

Directions: Follow the words across the elephant tracks. Write them in a sentence.

This   one   has   no   trunk.

This one has no trunk.

22

23

Directions: Find and circle the words in the box. Words can go → or ↓.

about
me
no
this
do

| t h i s f |
| s t m e o |
| a b o u t |
| n o t h i |
| u m y d l |
| b o r o e |

Directions: Write the missing word in each sentence.

1. I know **about** turtles.

2. **Do** you know about turtles?

3. **This** turtle is happy.

4. Will it bite **me** ?

5. **No**, it will not bite you!

Directions: Say each word as you trace it. Then, write each word on the line.

go   go

up   up

down   down

Directions: Turtle needs your help. Draw lines to connect the words that start with the same sound. Then, draw a turtle by your favorite words.

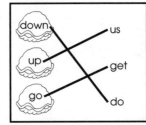

down   us

up   get

go   do

24

25

Directions: Color the spaces that have the same word as the one in the middle of the circle.

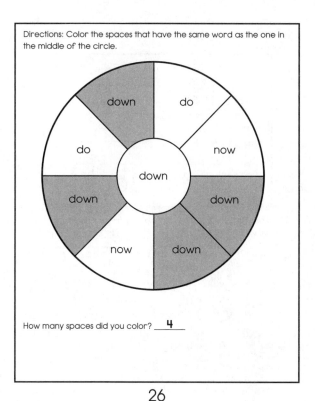

How many spaces did you color? __4__

26

Directions: Say each word as you trace it. Then, write each word on the line.

who   who

has   has

Directions: Read this sentence aloud. Then, write it on the line: **Who has the stick?**

Who has the stick?

Directions: Color the boxes that have the words **who** and **has** in them:

who	have	we	has
has	we	who	have
who	has	we	has
have	who	has	who

27

Directions: Read the words in the box. Find and circle the birthday cakes that have the words **who** and **has** on them.

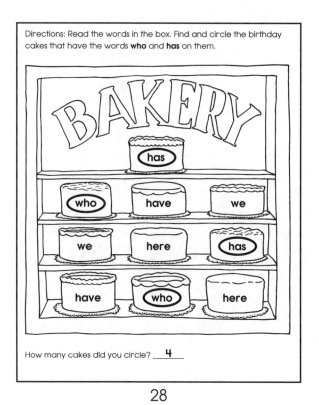

How many cakes did you circle? __4__

28

Directions: Say each word as you trace it. Then, write each word on the line.

are   are

put   put

Directions: Circle the two words in each row that are the same.

put	put	pet	pat
out	our	out	over
are	at	art	are
and	an	am	and

Directions: Say the words as you write this question: **Where did you put the car?**

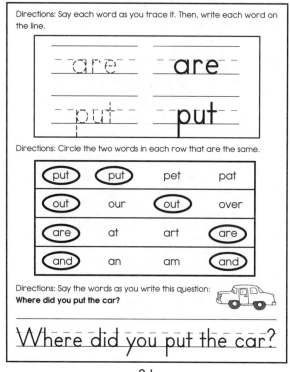

Where did you put the car?

31

Directions: Help the monkey find the bananas with **are** and **put**. Circle those bananas.

are	put

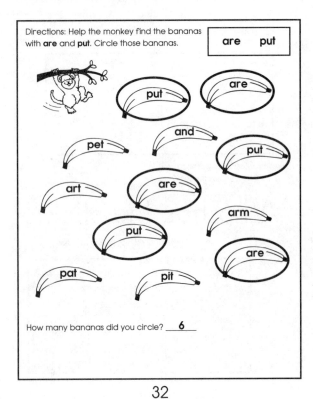

How many bananas did you circle? __6__

32

Directions: Say each word as you trace it. Then, write each word on the line.

in   in
on   on
out   out

Directions: Find and circle the fish that have **in**, **on**, and **out** on them.

in	on	out

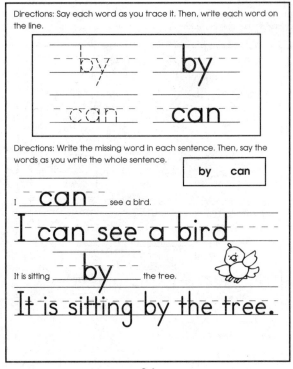

How many fish did you circle? __9__

33

Directions: Color the spaces that have the same word as the one in the middle of the circle.

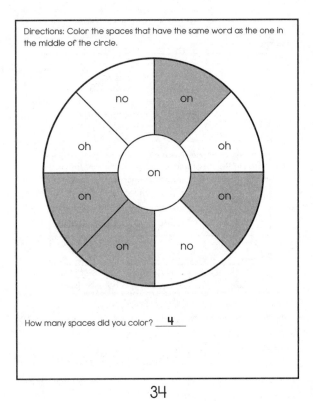

How many spaces did you color? __4__

34

Directions: Say each word as you trace it. Then, write each word on the line.

by   by
can   can

Directions: Write the missing word in each sentence. Then, say the words as you write the whole sentence.

by	can

I ___can___ see a bird.

I can see a bird

It is sitting ___by___ the tree.

It is sitting by the tree.

36

Directions: Find and circle the apples that have **by** and **can** on them.

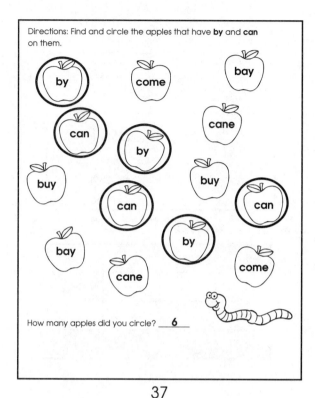

How many apples did you circle? ___6___

37

Directions: Write the words from the box on the lines.

| what | you | make |

what you make

Directions: The word **what** is hiding in the rows below. It can go → or ↓. Find and circle it.

t	h	a	t	h	h	e	t
w	h	a	t	h	e	a	e
h	t	a	w	a	h	t	w
a	w	h	a	t	w	a	h
w	h	e	a	h	t	w	a
h	a	w	h	a	t	h	t

38

Directions: Color the spaces that have the same word as the one in the middle of the circle.

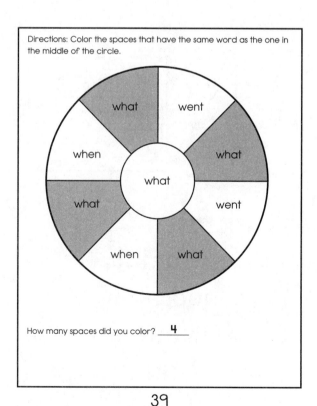

How many spaces did you color? ___4___

39

Directions: Write each word from the box on a line.

| an | good |

an good

Directions: The word **good** is hiding below. It can go → or ↓. Find and circle it.

g	o	n	e	g	o	n
o	n	e	g	o	o	g
o	g	o	n	o	n	o
d	o	g	e	d	o	o
g	o	o	d	n	o	d
d	o	n	g	o	o	d

How many times did you find it? ___5___

41

Answer Key

Directions: Say each word as you trace it. Then, write each word on the line.

an   **an**

good   **good**

Directions: Circle the two words in each row that are the same.

(an)	and	am	(an)
(you)	your	(you)	yes
(at)	ate	eat	(at)
(good)	give	gone	(good)

Directions: Say the words as you write this question:
Can you make a pie that is good?

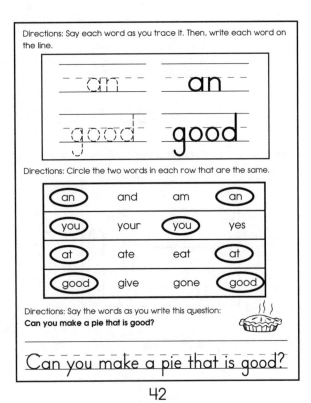

Can you make a pie that is good?

42

Directions: Say each word as you trace it. Then, write each word on the line.

at   **at**

eat   **eat**

get   **get**

Directions: Color the boxes that have **at**, **eat**, and **get** in them. Use a different color for each word.

get	an	at	go
gone	ate	the	get
ate	eat	got	and
at	get	eat	at

43

Directions: Say the word **eat** as you trace it. Then, write it on the line. Circle the foods that you like to eat.

eat   **eat**

Answers will vary.

Which is your favorite food? Write a sentence about it. Then, read your sentence aloud.

I like

Answers will vary.

44

Directions: Find and circle the words in the box. Words can go → or ↓.

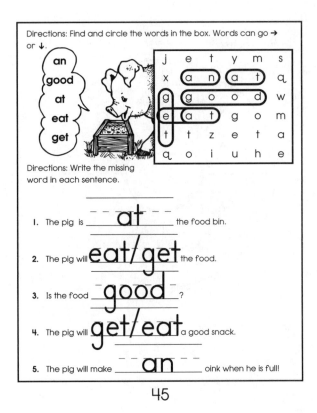

Directions: Write the missing word in each sentence.

1. The pig is ____**at**____ the food bin.

2. The pig will ____**eat/get**____ the food.

3. Is the food ____**good**____?

4. The pig will ____**get/eat**____ a good snack.

5. The pig will make ____**an**____ oink when he is full!

45

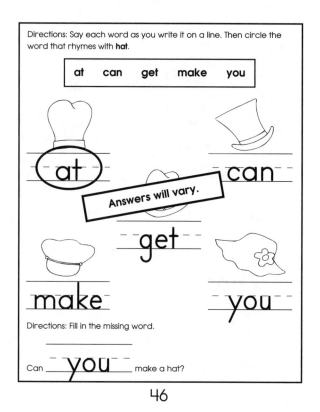

Directions: Say each word as you write it on a line. Then circle the word that rhymes with **hat**.

| at | can | get | make | you |

at   can

Answers will vary.

get

make   you

Directions: Fill in the missing word.

Can __you__ make a hat?

46

Directions: Find and circle the hearts that have **give** and **from** on them.

How many did you circle?   give __4__   from __4__

47

Directions: Say each word as you trace it. Then, write each word on the line.

give   give
from   from

Directions: Circle the two words in each row that are the same.

can	cat	car	can
from	four	from	for
ate	eat	at	ate
give	good	gone	give

Directions: Say the words as you write this sentence:
Give him the note from me.

Dear Jack,
I will see you after school.
Love, Mom

Give him the note from me.

48

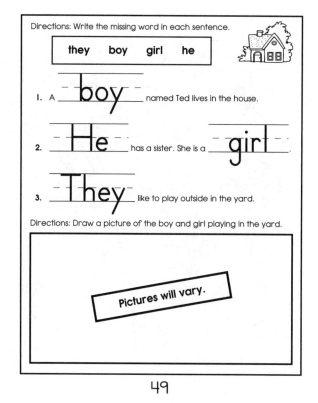

Directions: Write the missing word in each sentence.

| they | boy | girl | he |

1. A __boy__ named Ted lives in the house.

2. __He__ has a sister. She is a __girl__

3. __They__ like to play outside in the yard.

Directions: Draw a picture of the boy and girl playing in the yard.

Pictures will vary.

49

Directions: Color the spaces that have the same word as the one in the middle of the circle.

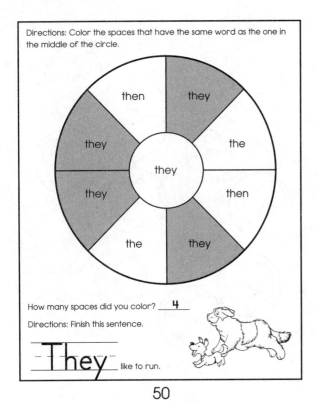

How many spaces did you color? __4__

Directions: Finish this sentence.

They like to run.

50

Directions: Find and circle the words in the box. Words can go → or ↓.

give
from
they
boy
girl
he

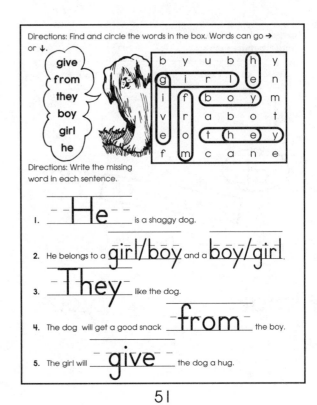

Directions: Write the missing word in each sentence.

1. __He__ is a shaggy dog.

2. He belongs to a __girl/boy__ and a __boy/girl__.

3. __They__ like the dog.

4. The dog will get a good snack __from__ the boy.

5. The girl will __give__ the dog a hug.

51

Directions: Find and circle the sheep that have the words **she** and **then** on them.

| she | then |

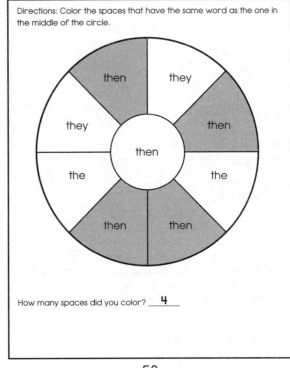

How many did you circle? __6__

52

Directions: Color the spaces that have the same word as the one in the middle of the circle.

then | they
they | then
then
the | the
then | then

How many spaces did you color? __4__

53

Directions: Say each word as you trace it. Then, write each word on the line.

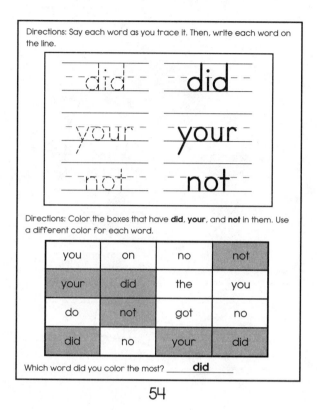

Directions: Color the boxes that have **did**, **your**, and **not** in them. Use a different color for each word.

you	on	no	not
your	did	the	you
do	not	got	no
did	no	your	did

Which word did you color the most? _____ **did** _____

54

Directions: Find and circle the ice cream cones with **did**, **your**, and **not** on them.

did	your	not

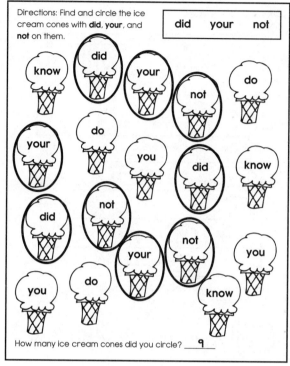

How many ice cream cones did you circle? _____ **9**

55

Directions: Find and circle the words in the box. Words can go → or ↓.

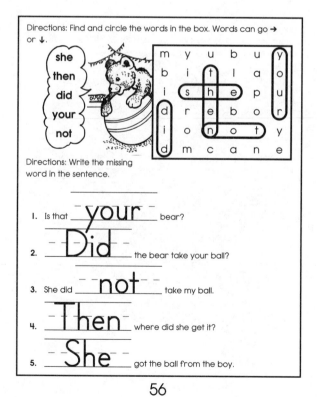

Directions: Write the missing word in the sentence.

1. Is that _**your**_ bear?

2. _**Did**_ the bear take your ball?

3. She did _**not**_ take my ball.

4. _**Then**_ where did she get it?

5. _**She**_ got the ball from the boy.

56

Directions: Say each word as you write it on a line.

she	they	give
eat	boy	

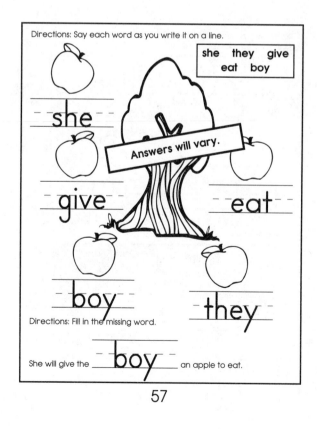

she

give   eat

Answers will vary.

boy   they

Directions: Fill in the missing word.

She will give the _**boy**_ an apple to eat.

57

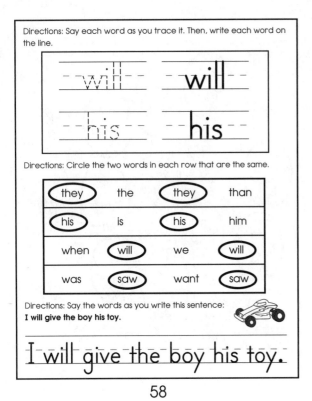

Directions: Say each word as you trace it. Then, write each word on the line.

will   will

his   his

Directions: Circle the two words in each row that are the same.

(they)	the	(they)	than
(his)	is	(his)	him
when	(will)	we	(will)
was	(saw)	want	(saw)

Directions: Say the words as you write this sentence:
I will give the boy his toy.

I will give the boy his toy.

58

Directions: Color the spaces that have the same word as the one in the middle of the circle.

his	his
this	this
his	*his*	him
him	his

Directions: Write a sentence using the word in the middle of the circle.

Sentences will vary.

59

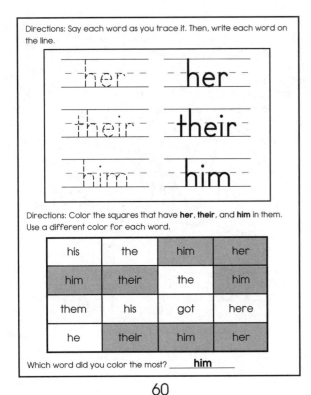

Directions: Say each word as you trace it. Then, write each word on the line.

her   her

their   their

him   him

Directions: Color the squares that have **her**, **their**, and **him** in them. Use a different color for each word.

his	the	him	her
him	their	the	him
them	his	got	here
he	their	him	her

Which word did you color the most? ____**him**____

60

Directions: Find and circle the turtles that have the words **her**, **their**, and **him** on them.

| her | their | him |

How many turtles did you circle? ___**8**___

61

Answer Key

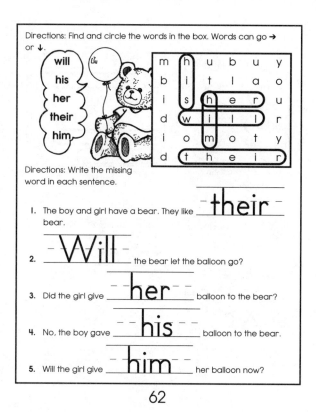

Directions: Find and circle the words in the box. Words can go → or ↓.

will
his
her
their
him

```
m  h  u  b  u  y
b  i  t  l  a  o
i  s  h  e  r  u
d  i  w  i  l  l  r
i  o  m  o  t  y
d  t  h  e  i  r
```

Directions: Write the missing word in each sentence.

1. The boy and girl have a bear. They like __their__ bear.

2. __Will__ the bear let the balloon go?

3. Did the girl give __her__ balloon to the bear?

4. No, the boy gave __his__ balloon to the bear.

5. Will the girl give __him__ her balloon now?

62

Directions: Say each word as you trace it. Then, write each word on the line.

them   them
know   know

Directions: The words **them** and **know** are hiding in the lines below. Find and circle them.

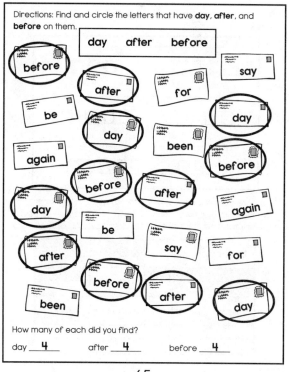

them

t h h e m (t h e m) t h e e t h m

know

k n o n w (k n o w) n o w k n e

63

Directions: Color the spaces that have the same word as the one in the middle of the circle.

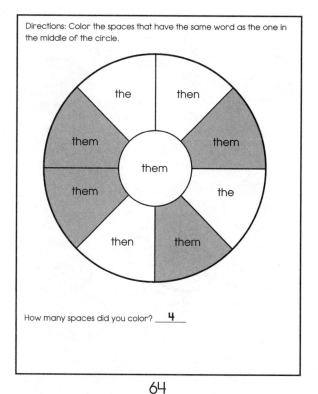

the | then | them | them | them | the | then | them

them

How many spaces did you color? __4__

64

Directions: Find and circle the letters that have **day**, **after**, and **before** on them.

day   after   before

before
after   for
be   day   say
day   been   day
again   before
before   after
day   again
be   say
after   for
before   after
been   before   day

How many of each did you find?

day __4__   after __4__   before __4__

65

Spectrum Sight Words
Grade K

Answer Key

151

Directions: Say each word as you trace it. Then, write each word on the line.

day   **day**

after   **after**

before   **before**

Directions: Circle the two words in each row that are the same.

(day)	date	(day)	dart
(before)	begin	been	(before)
(after)	ate	often	(after)
(go)	got	gone	(go)

Directions: Say the words as you write this sentence:
Go the day after today.

Go the day after today.

66

Directions: Find and circle the words in the box. Words can go → or ↓.

them
know
day
after
before

k	n	t	h	e	m
b	e	f	o	r	e
a	d	a	t	t	d
y	e	s	h	h	a
a	f	t	e	r	y
k	n	o	w	n	s

Directions: Write the missing word in each sentence.

1. Do you __know__ about penguins?

2. What do you know about __them__?

3. __Before__ they swim, they jump in the water.

4. __After__ they swim, they can rest.

5. It is a long __day__ for them!

67

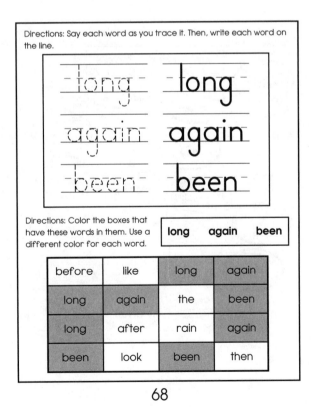

Directions: Say each word as you trace it. Then, write each word on the line.

long   **long**

again   **again**

been   **been**

Directions: Color the boxes that have these words in them. Use a different color for each word.

long   again   been

before	like	long	again
long	again	the	been
long	after	rain	again
been	look	been	then

68

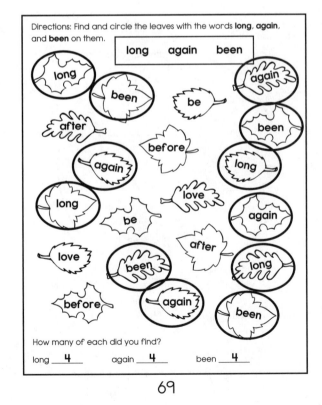

Directions: Find and circle the leaves with the words **long**, **again**, and **been** on them.

long   again   been

How many of each did you find?

long __4__   again __4__   been __4__

69

Directions: Say each word as you trace it. Then, write each word on the line.

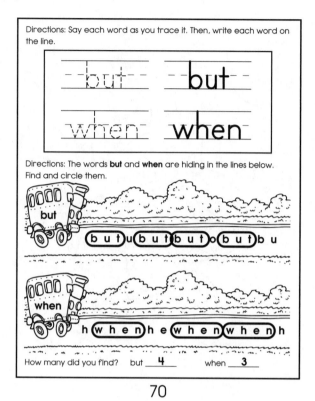

Directions: The words **but** and **when** are hiding in the lines below. Find and circle them.

How many did you find?   but __4__   when __3__

70

Directions: Color the spaces that have the same word as the one in the middle of the circle.

How many spaces did you color? __4__

71

Directions: Find and circle the words in the box. Words can go → or ↓.

long
again
been
but
when

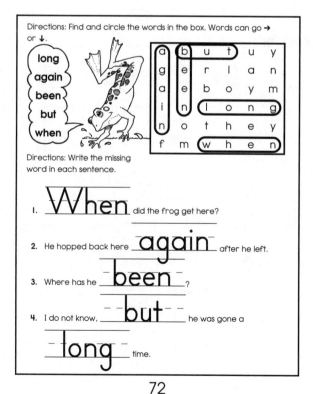

Directions: Write the missing word in each sentence.

1. __When__ did the frog get here?

2. He hopped back here __again__ after he left.

3. Where has he __been__ ?

4. I do not know, __but__ he was gone a __long__ time.

72

Directions: Say each word as you write it on a line.

been	long	when	they	on

Answers will vary.

been   long

when

they   on

Directions: Fill in the missing word:

They have been __on__ a long ride.

73

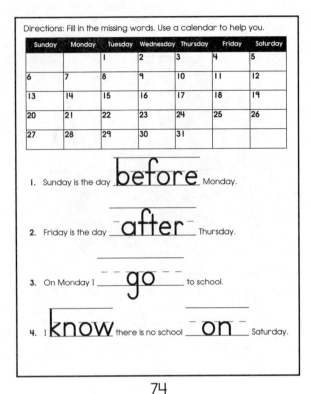

Directions: Fill in the missing words. Use a calendar to help you.

Sunday	Monday	Tuesday	Wednesday	Thursday	Friday	Saturday
		1	2	3	4	5
6	7	8	9	10	11	12
13	14	15	16	17	18	19
20	21	22	23	24	25	26
27	28	29	30	31		

1. Sunday is the day **before** Monday.

2. Friday is the day **after** Thursday.

3. On Monday I **go** to school.

4. I **know** there is no school **on** Saturday.

74

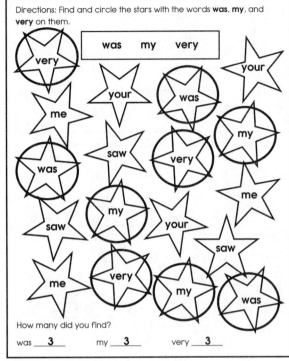

Directions: Find and circle the stars with the words **was**, **my**, and **very** on them.

was   my   very

How many did you find?

was __3__   my __3__   very __3__

75

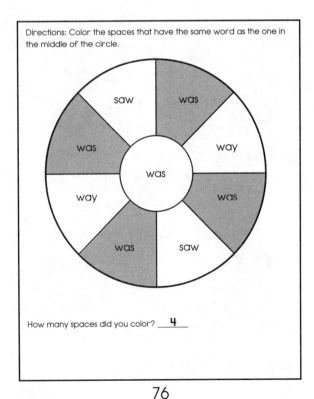

Directions: Color the spaces that have the same word as the one in the middle of the circle.

How many spaces did you color? __4__

76

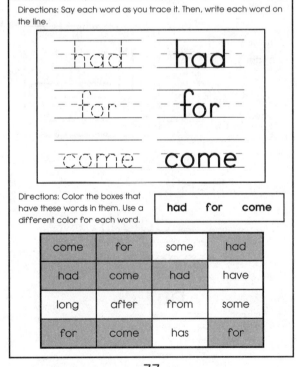

Directions: Say each word as you trace it. Then, write each word on the line.

had   had
for   for
come   come

Directions: Color the boxes that have these words in them. Use a different color for each word.

had   for   come

come	for	some	had
had	come	had	have
long	after	from	some
for	come	has	for

77

Directions: Find and circle the words in the box. Words can go → or ↓.

was
my
very
had
for
come

b	y	u	b	(m	y)
c	o	m	e	a	(w
(v	f	o	r)	y	a
e	h	a	b	o	s)
r	o	t	(h	a	d)
y	m	c	a	n	e

Directions: Write the missing word in each sentence.

1. This is ___my___ fish.

2. He is my ___very___ favorite fish. He ___was___ little when I got him.

3. When I feed him, he will ___come___ to the top of the tank.

78

Directions: Say each word as you trace it. Then, write each word on the line.

be

of

that

Directions: Circle the two words in each row that are the same.

been	(be)	but	(be)
if	on	(of)	(of)
at	(that)	(that)	ate
have	(has)	his	(has)

Directions: Say the words as you write this sentence: **It is king of the jungle.**

It is king of the jungle.

79

Directions: Find and circle the flowers with the words **be**, **of**, and **that** on them.

| be | of | that |

if · of · that · if · be · then · been · if · that · been · of · be · then · been · of · that · then · be

How many did you find?

be __3__   of __3__   that __3__

80

Directions: Say each word as you trace it. Then, write each word on the line.

were

if

would

Directions: Color the boxes that have these words in them. Use a different color for each word.

| were | if | would |

was	for	would	if
if	for	of	have
long	would	from	where
of	were	has	for

How many did you find?

were __1__   if __2__   would __2__

81

Answer Key

Directions: Color the spaces that have the same word as the one in the middle of the circle.

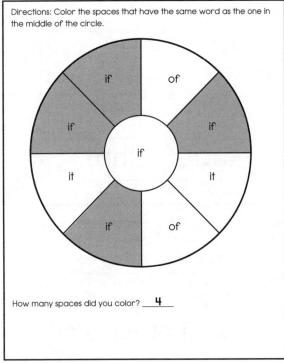

How many spaces did you color? __4__

82

Directions: Say each word as you trace it. Then, write each word on the line.

just   just

there   there

so   so

Directions: Circle the two words in each row that are the same.

on	one	so	so
just	jeep	just	jump
then	there	the	there
was	were	went	were

Directions: Say the words as you write this sentence:
There are so many dogs!

There are so many dogs!

84

Directions: Find and circle the pumpkins with the words **just**, **there**, and **so** on them.

just   there   so

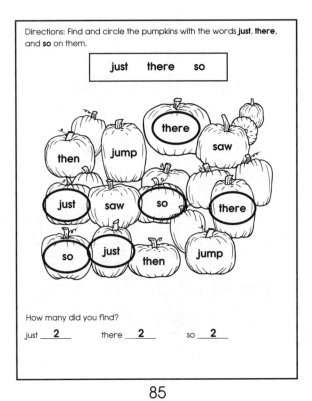

How many did you find?

just __2__   there __2__   so __2__

85

Directions: Say each word as you trace it. Then, write each word on the line.

little   little

or   or

with   with

Directions: Help the duck find the words that start with the same letter. Draw a line to connect the words that match. Draw a baby duck by your favorite words.

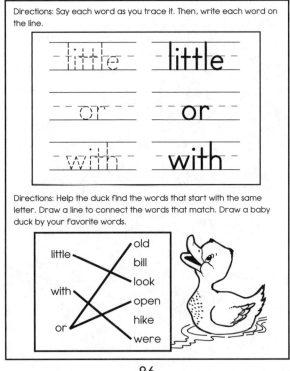

86

Directions: Color the spaces that have the same word as the one in the middle of the circle.

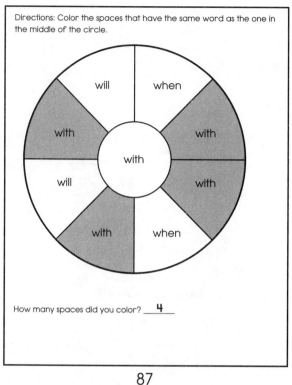

How many spaces did you color? __4__

87

Directions: Find and circle the words in the box. Words can go → or ↓.

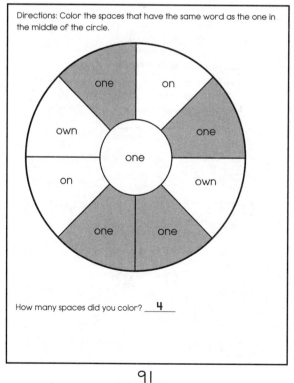

Directions: Write each missing word in the sentences.

1. **There** is a **little** mouse.

2. Is he there **with** a piece of cheese?

3. Is he brown **or** gray?

4. Why is he **so** little?

5. He is **just** a baby.

88

Directions: Say each word as you trace it. Then, write each word on the line.

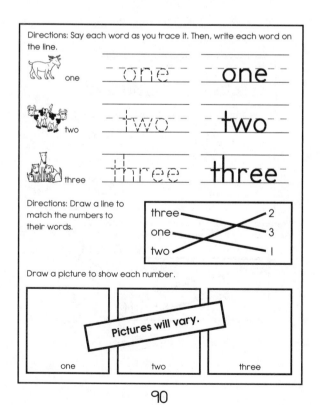

one   one   one

two   two   two

three   three   three

Directions: Draw a line to match the numbers to their words.

three — 2
one — 3
two — 1

Draw a picture to show each number.

Pictures will vary.

one   two   three

90

Directions: Color the spaces that have the same word as the one in the middle of the circle.

one   on
own   one
one
on   own
one   one

How many spaces did you color? __4__

91

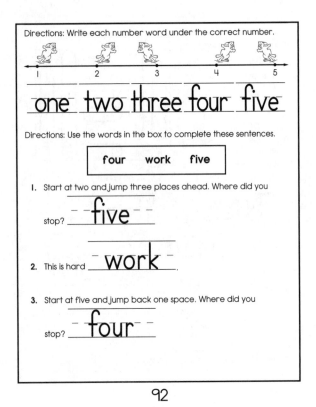

Directions: Write each number word under the correct number.

one two three four five

Directions: Use the words in the box to complete these sentences.

| four | work | five |

1. Start at two and jump three places ahead. Where did you stop? __five__

2. This is hard __work__.

3. Start at five and jump back one space. Where did you stop? __four__

92

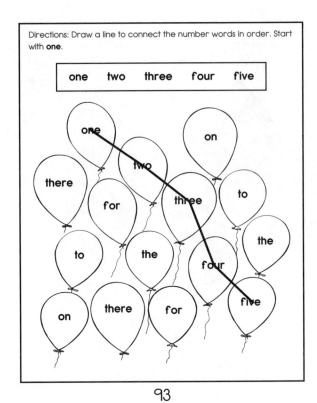

Directions: Draw a line to connect the number words in order. Start with **one**.

| one | two | three | four | five |

93

Directions: Write the correct number word on each line.

one two three four five

1 __one__   2 __two__

3 __three__

4 __four__   5 __five__

94

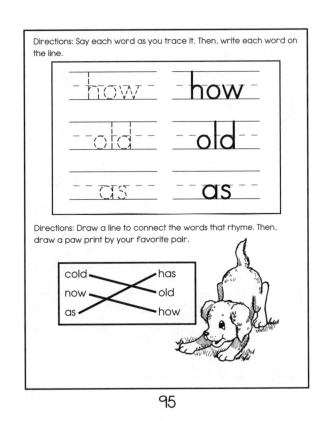

Directions: Say each word as you trace it. Then, write each word on the line.

how   how

old   old

as   as

Directions: Draw a line to connect the words that rhyme. Then, draw a paw print by your favorite pair.

cold — has
now — old
as — how

95

Page 96

Directions: Read and answer the questions below.

1. How old are you?

_____

- - - - - - - -

I am _____ years old.

2. Draw candles on the cake to show how old you are.

3. How old will you be next year?

Answers will vary.

I will be _____ years old.

4. Draw a picture of a present that you want for your birthday.

5. How tall will you be?

_____

- - - - - - - -

I will be as tall as a _____ .

96

Page 97

Directions: Say each word as you trace it. Then, write each word on the line.

said   said

take   take

some   some

Directions: Color the boxes that have these words in them. Use a different color for each word.

said   take   some

take	then	said	some
so	take	the	she
the	two	take	that
said	some	said	some

97

Page 98

Directions: Find and circle the eggs with the words **said**, **take**, and **some** on them.

said   take   some

said   make   some

did   take   come

some   said   take

come   make   did

How many eggs did you circle?

said __2__   take __2__   some __2__

98

Page 99

Directions: Find and circle the words in the box. Words can go → or ↓.

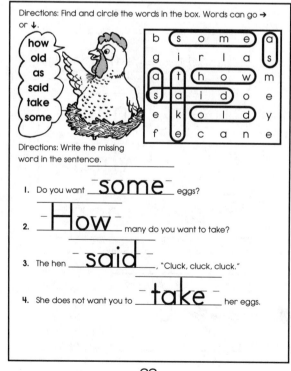

how
old
as
said
take
some

b	s	o	m	e	a
g	i	r	l	a	s
a	t	h	o	w	m
s	a	i	d	o	e
e	k	o	l	d	y
f	e	c	a	n	e

Directions: Write the missing word in the sentence.

1. Do you want **some** eggs?

2. **How** many do you want to take?

3. The hen **said** , "Cluck, cluck, cluck."

4. She does not want you to **take** her eggs.

99

Directions: Say each word as you trace it. Then, write each word on the line.

other other

any any

much much

Directions: Draw a line to connect the words that rhyme.

other — many
any — such
much — mother

100

Directions: Color the spaces that have the same word as the one in the middle of the circle.

any | an
an | any
any | my
my | any

(middle: any)

How many times did you find the word **any**? __4__

What other words did you find? **an, my**

101

Directions: Say each word as you trace it. Then, write each word on the line.

many many

new new

which which

man man

Directions: Draw a line to connect the words that start with the same sound.

which — me
new — make
man — not
many — when

102

Directions: Find and circle the mittens with the words from the box on them.

many   new   which   man

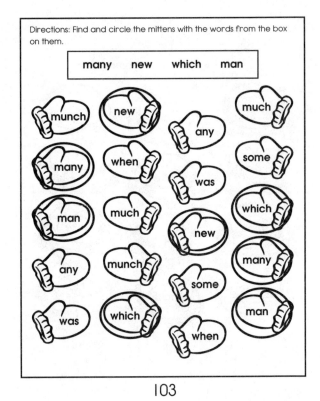

103